J; Bagshawe

Daily Reflections 2007

Edited by Angela Fairbrace & Michelle Afford

forwardpress

First published in Great Britain in 2007 by:
Forward Press Ltd.
Remus House
Coltsfoot Drive
Peterborough
PE2 9JX
Telephone: 01733 898108
Website: www.forwardpress.co.uk

SB ISBN 978-1 84418 470 5

Foreword

Although we are a nation of poets we are accused of not reading poetry, or buying poetry books. After many years of listening to the incessant gripes of poetry publishers, I can only assume that the books they publish, in general, are books that most people do not want to read.

Poetry should not be obscure, introverted, and as cryptic as a crossword puzzle: it is the poet's duty to reach out and embrace the world.

The world owes the poet nothing and we should not be expected to dig and delve into a rambling discourse searching for some inner meaning.

The reason we write poetry (and almost all of us do) is because we want to communicate: an ideal; an idea; or a specific feeling. Poetry is as essential in communication, as a letter; a radio; a telephone, and the main criterion for selecting the poems in this anthology is very simple: they communicate.

Contents

The Poems

A White Lily For Me

White lilies fragrance
surrounding the place
their beauty adding a magical touch
I walk between them
with my white dress
my wedding night
looking happy and bright
like I've wings
lilies so soft surrounding me
losing myself between them
this night is for me and my prince
the lilies celebrating with us
what a lovely touch
oh baby, I love you so much
ever since you handed me the white lily
since then I've had for you an endless crush
a white lily is our love symbol
screaming it loud to all people
a lovely dream I had
me, you and the lily
that made me glad
a dream I wish would come true
it was our wedding
me and you.

Yassmin Elnazer

Tomorrow Is Another Day

When forlorn and feeling low
And all appears pointless to you;
Think of the days of long ago
When in your past the joys you knew.

I look and wonder at the sight
Of all the roses, large and small,
Filling the air of smell; delight!
Uplifts my spirit from the fall.

Although it's hard to take advice
And lift one's self from feeling down,
Thoughts of happy days will suffice
To erase and replace the frown.

We all have happy memories
And diff'rent ways to cheer us up.
We all have had some revelries
Of tales of fun and wine to sup!

So shed the gloom and smile again,
Within yourself start an affray;
Treat all negatives with disdain!
Tomorrow is another day!

William Barnard

Field's Edge

There is a path where no one goes.
Only the deer, rabbits and foxes roam.
Grand ancient oak trees for its roof;
Centuries of leaf mould for its loam.

Plank bridges, pondweed and dew pools
And sluggish meandering streams.
Wooden stiles and dripping brambles;
Winding paths leading to our dreams.

Overhanging branches form the
Tunnel of dark as it winds
To the deer plunge in the wood.
Beaten back grasses are the only signs.

Deep down in darkly hidden depths,
Green velvet mosses carpet rutted bark.
High in the trees a wind whisper.
In sweetest song soars the skylark.

Secret leaf-soft paths where yews knarl
To grottoes that drip with dew so sweet
That feed dark pools where deer
Slake the thirst of summer heat.

Yellow blooms like wax slivers blaze
As floral gymkhana rosettes.
Baby moorhens with massive feet
Walk on lily-padded carpets.

Full-eared wheat teems with butterflies.
Nestlings fledge and black beetles crawl.
Nature holds her balance just right
And the brown buzzard watches all.

Joan Woolley

Grandad

I loved to sit on Grandad's knee
Tales were what he told to me
He talked of places far and wide
I'd snuggle at times, my face to hide
He talked of legends and of myths
At Christmas Wise Men and their gifts
He showed me all the stars at night
And all the planets shining bright
We looked at photos of Ma and Pa
Plus many more of Great Grandma
He talked about when he worked the farm
My grandad was a man with charm
Grandad I knew would always love me
I loved him so very much you see
My memories begin from when I was three
I loved to sit on Grandad's knee.

Dawn Bennie

I'm Not Alone

When I'm lonely or depressed
When I worry about
The ins and outs
Of living life
When I'm stressed
And nothing seems to be
Going right for me
The thing that keeps me sane
Is the knowledge that
I'm not alone in this world
And my troubles are minuscule
When compared with others.

Nayyar Shabbir Ahmad

Five-Thirty Blues And Gold

Only just five-thirty am.
The day was yet a babe.
Though lying awake for an hour or so,
Decisions were already laid.

But why this brief uncertainty?
Was it indeed much more?
Too aware we have no control at all,
Might this be another closed door?

Dull pain was already speaking,
Just like a trusted friend!
But his feigning could never deceive me
Or life completely upend.

To sleep in peace set free from him,
Would be such luxury.
His intrusion, all too familiar;
His dark intention plain to see.

The silence almost deafening
As life's thoughts crowded in.
Reality is not always easy,
While the world still enquires 'Whose sin?'

So cut to the chase, don't linger!
No sin committed here.
But that our advocates grace and glory,
Should be manifested and clear.

So what stops one from going mad?
There's nothing without hope.
And hope springs eternal through faith alone,
True faith never runs out of rope.

The thermostat is in good hands,
The furnace will glow cold!
For all those that persist and walk in faith,
Will emerge more precious than gold!

Kent Brooksbank

Breaking Silence

I feel I have been silenced for too long.
I want to go
where grass is green
and mountains rise up echoing
to shout your love
in rainbow tones
know it rebounding, journeying on,
or source a wandering, whispering stream
that gathers pace
and flows on ceaselessly,
exposing you through me,
the great unknown.

Nancy Charley

Summer Sunset Comes To Kerrera

Summer sunset
Comes to Kerrera.

Light chases shadow
Up the rugged slopes,
Turning the grey to flashes
Of vivid green,

Dies across
The sound of Mull
Behind deep
Plum-purple mountains.

Nightfall
Simplifies the island
To a dark outline.

When I see this
I am always amazed
How the spirit
Speaks to the heart.

Tim Hoare

Christmas Praise

On a Christmas morning
Just before dawn,
In the blackness a bird sang,
Just one,
Yet his notes grew
And music spilled from him,
On and on
Until the whole sky seemed
Filled with his song.

On that first Christmas
In the lit-up sky
Above a sheep scattered hill,
The song of the angels
Could not have filled
The heavens with more joy.

Karen Wood

The Life In The Seed

You found an old packet of lettuce seeds left over from last year
whilst planting out this season's salad leaves.

The packet was battered and faded and the seeds
                                    all dry and shrivelled
but you put them in anyway, in neat little drills, in a spare planting tray.

Placing it with the others prepared in the same way
you gave it a wry smile thinking that it was probably
                                    a waste of time and effort
but you watered it anyway.

As you checked on the progress of your planted seeds
over the next few weeks you noticed all the other trays
had started to show signs of growth with small seedlings
peeping through the prepared compost
emerging there with confidence and rooted well.

The old lettuce seeds however remained resolutely dormant -
no paired green leaflets, no slender stems, no vital signs.

Time to plant out the tomatoes already
in a patch alongside the bushing broad beans
whose thick stems and dark dotted flowers
hold the prospect of a healthy crop later on in the season.

Then, unexpectedly, whilst clearing away the empty tomato trays
whose former tenants are now safely watered into the good earth
you become aware of a belated greening of lettuce seedlings
which was not there the previous day.

Twin green leaves on pale spindly stems are spread across the tray
as they absorb the nutrients at their feet and rise to greet
the mingled scents of early summer and warming days
in the almost empty potting shed.

As I wash and dry the unfurled leaves of a fine Webb's lettuce
picked some weeks later, I smile
as I reflect upon this vegetable's modest demonstration
of the ebb and flow of the tides and the cycle of the seasons,
its timely resurrection, and the prospect of its imminent transmutation -
in my Caesar salad!

Maureen Horne

Bright Blue Skies

It's as if it is the voice of an angel
every time I hear you call my name
my heart lifts high
the heavy grey clouds disperse
replaced by those bright and blue
'cause of the love you unsparingly give

every breath that I take is
a dedication to you I make
it makes me want to skip and dance
live life to the full
come forward from the stern
no longer looking back at yesterday

the cloak of darkness removed
pain of a wounded heart repaired
as we gather together and share our love
I may be old fashioned
by some considered square
sit on a chair and not the floor

work my corner and care
for the poor and wayward soul
step back when plaudits appear
applaud the efforts of others
hold out my hand least they slip and fall
and ever awake to my master's call.

Maurice Hope

The Kingdom Of Peace

Still your heart and mind
And unite with Me in silence
The vibrant silence of your soul
Let all earthy sounds and distractions
Dissolve into a deep nothingness
To rest within My very being
Where you are at one with creation
Come, enter My kingdom of peace
A place of beauty beyond Man's comprehension
Where the stars play a symphony of joy
Joy and expectations of that which is to come
A place of beauty where sadness and failure
Are without substance or existence
In that divine consummation
You are truly united with infinity
Encapsulated in the warmth of My love
A gift freely given to all.

Wilma Hogg

Find It Where You Will

Let the power of the spirit bathe your wounds
The silent words of prayer carry healing
You can wake the dreamer
But the dream will go on - go on - go on.
Silent
    Gentle
        Drifting
Loss stays
Hurt goes on - and on
So much is out of reach
But only of my dreaming, not of the spirit
So much not yet understood
How many tears do I cry not seen
Beyond moon - sun - and stars
So much to challenge my strength, my calm
I know - only I can know
The inner hunger needs to be filled
So please know my friend
That there is a light to guide us all
And the wind is born of a breeze
Leaping flames likewise from a spark
Find power where you will
And hope in every new step.

Clive Cornwall

Sunshine

The sun shines upon me;
Gladdening my heart.
Lifting my pall
Of trouble and sadness.
Carrying me upwards
To cloud-free heights.

The whole earth is responding;
Drawn upward in gladness;
Strong rays of sun
Pierce the Earth's deep core.
So flowers are unfolding
And tree buds appear.

Whence this wonderful power
That brings resurrection,
That awakens all life
To burgeon and blossom?
The sun, God's possession,
Joy and life gives to all.

Mary Johnson-Riley

Tranquil Moments

Perchance to lay beneath the trees
Amidst the gentle rustling leaves;
With summer's soothing balmy breeze
And languish peacefully at ease.

To while away the endless hours
Smelling lovely fragrant flowers;
And even with the summer showers
Relish all of nature's powers.

To ponder careless by a stream
Where sun-kissed gurgling waters gleam;
Which from each dazzling rainbow beam
Induce hypnotic thoughts to dream.

To gaze at seagulls as they fly
On warm air currents up on high;
So free and easy in the sky
With lazy grace they drift and cry.

To sit beside a lapping sea
Where rippling rhythmic waves can be,
A balm that sets fraught feelings free
In moments of tranquillity.

To watch with wonder as the sun
Sinks out of sight when day is done,
And radiant splendour sure to stun
Before another day's begun.

Bill Newham

Party

A beautiful garden surrounded by trees
Sometimes the sun, but sometimes a breeze

The table is covered with a bright cloth
The trifle is covered with foamy white froth

But before I can taste it we all make a toast
A drink to our friends, a drink to our host

The food is laid out on a big oak square
Salads, meats, puddings, wonderful fare

Then after the feasting we might play a game
Rounders I think with the bat as a flame

Like Olympians in training, who would have thought
Anyone one might make it if they are taught!

I refer to friendships, food and fun
Come on now don't sit but run!

Barbara Tozer

Relax! Put Your Feet Up!

Relax! Put your feet up - you deserve a break!
Time out from your busy schedule you can surely take,
Why not sit in your favourite chair
And pick up the book that's lying there?

I know you're eager to take a look inside,
Its gripping tale will make your eyes grow wide;
You'll be transported to a world far away,
But from your seat you won't need to stray!

Everything around you may be quiet and still,
But happiness will abound, you'll get your fill;
The plot you'll picture in your mind's eye,
You'll be so engrossed that time will fly!

Moments like these provide such a sweet repose
As you smile and revel in the story you chose;
Journeys into the world of literature make you feel rich
And it's the only kind of travel where there's never a hitch!

So I think I might sit down beside you
And enjoy a spot of reading too.

Annabelle Tipper

Air Transcends

Air transcends into oblivion
Like the way you drift to me
In this simple moment of freedom
Try to find my melody

Have you ever had your heart broken
And questioned your sanity
Then let me show you your potential
Let me be your therapy

Not sure how to answer the question
Take an opportunity
To sleep on the concept overnight
You'll find love is all you need

As vertigo passes, it opens
To the shifting harmony
In hopes that you gave a second thought
To this possibility

S Morris

The Sun Is Shining

The sun is shining, hip hip hooray
The rain has finally gone away.
'I'm going out Mum. Out to play,'
There's no more rain out there today.

I could bounce on my hopper;
Ride my Raleigh Chopper;
Eat a big gobstopper;
And climb.

Jump into a puddle;
Gather in a huddle;
Get all in a muddle;
What's time?

The sun is shining, hip hip hooray!
The rain has finally gone away.
Clouds, just shapes that help me play,
There's no more rain out here today.

Robert West

The Stuff That Dreams Are Made Of
(To Gulliver)

I live the dreams you dream
in wasted night-long sleeps.
Death rather than that!
Without sleep, they say,
you live very little.

Like Dante's 'Divine Comedy',
dreams arouse fantasy.
Nightmares come to life
in night's deep shadows,
crawl lightly into the feathers
of your soft pillows,
those you bang every morning
while hating yourself for remembering
or forgetting dreams.

Fatigue and rest are opium -
close your eyes
and it's all over for that day.
Sunset, fast-forwarded is within you:
enter the world of adventure!
Sunrise is folded in a curtain,
at the command of your alarm clock.

Open your eyes, look inward,
there is no rest in slumber,
only in dreams.
The child becomes Hercules,
Ursus, Ulysses, Perseus;
he fights, never dies -
under the sheets.

This is why I fly
whilst you fall, breaking your bones;
I see red in the darkness of anger,
white in refrigerated ice,
black in oblivion,
yellow in cowardly escapades;
but what the hell!

Like Gulliver
I live the dreams you dream
and deal with far worse monsters
than your everyday office routine.
I am not safe like you,
when you wake shaken by a nightmare;
for all the time my life is at stake,
whether asleep or awake,
like snowflakes, it can all vanish
on touchdown in the lake.

Raymond Fenech

You're Life

Surrounded by angels,
A kiss from above
Made by the Highest,
Made with true love

A long way to find,
But worth it for sure
He's watching your moves,
Giving you love so pure

You will find it nowhere,
How this feels deep inside
He will always take care,
He's the way and the light

Dreams He has given
Dreams in your heart
With Him it will happen,
In Him put your trust

He will answer your prayers,
It's you that He heard
'Cause big plans He made,
For your life on Earth.

Miriam Kluin

Always There

I never need to go that extra mile
Because you are always there
I need not stress and worry
For I know how deeply you care

My needs are never unfulfilled
Promises you always keep
Forever on my mind
Be I awake or be I asleep

My heart, it aches when we're apart
And soars when together again
With you it's not a case of never
Always a case of when?

To be without your love
Would to not be at all
My world it would vanish
My life would be so small

Your love gives us possibilities
Leading to avenues I thought didn't exist
The passion you stir within me
Ensures that you I can never resist

Elaine Donaldson

Lie And Lay

I want to lie . . . lay . . .
Lay down
For twenty minutes
Say you when again you
Confuse lie
With lay

The dishes lay
In the sink
With a smell of peanut butter
Coffee and bread
The clothes lay
On the floor above the shoes
Whose soles your warmth
And weight gently nip
Away
The dreams lay
Down closely to your bed
To arouse a few light tunes
After a long day

And here I lay
No . . . no . . .
You lay me down
To revolve around you
Like twin stars
Only
For your glow

David Lin

Under The Cherry Tree

From the window I could see
You running around without clothes
Under the cherry tree. Warm evening -
The sky . . . looking bruised.

Why you had decided to undress
And go outside when I wasn't looking,
No one knows -
Born with independence in mind.

Nearly three years old. A small . . . being
In this vast . . . nature -
In your own little world.
You felt free to do as you pleased.

I'll be . . . like me.
The moment was what mattered to you.
And the moment was good.
Clothes weren't necessary at all.

You loved playing, just living,
You loved your surroundings,
The feel of grass under your tiny feet.
Nothing was weighing on you, no one.

Free to be. I watched you running around -
I love you Max.
In my mind I still see you,
Living life without any constraints.

Watch me, Grannie, watch me!
A sort of wild . . . freedom,
A wonderful sunny face
And smile.

Claire-Lyse Sylvester

Take Time

If life and work leave you stressed
And then you start to get depressed.
Heavy shackles seem to bind you.
Take time to walk beneath tall trees,
Watch dappled sunlight dance on leaves,
And God's peace will find you.

If money problems get you down,
And worrying brings on a frown,
Then even sleep seems to elude you.
Take time to wander by a stream,
Enjoy the break, sit and dream,
And God's peace will soothe you.

When you think you just can't cope
Life's getting now beyond a joke.
And all the problems just confound you.
Take time to climb the highest hill,
Breathe in the view, the sky, be still,
And God's peace will surround you.

Gwen Hoskins

Step Lightly

Let the light fall slowly over the grassy fields,
Suburbia and the muddy weals,
Let the light fall, so eventide will bring
A glowing, starry interlude,
In a sky that shines to heal.
No matter how shadow chases
The spaces all between,
The light will always lift,
To hide the darkness in-between.
This light then, a dancing play of sun,
A golden orb to warm cold hearts
Ensures the dawn to come.
Then sorrows pale beside the waxing moon,
As silvery moonbeams dance
To a glorious chordant tune.

Glenda Stryker

Beneath This Old Oak Tree

The bluebells in the forest
The daisy in the glade
The tiny sweet anemone
Just nestling in the shade

The sweet song of the blackbird
As she busily makes her nest
The humming of the buzzing bee
The nectar sweet and fresh

Sitting in the summer sun
The children in the pool
What finer times are there in life
So why am I the fool?

To take upon the daily grind
Keeping up with modern times
The simplicity of nature's way
A million miles from my mind

It is only as I sit here
And tarry for a while
And take in all this wonder
That I have to sadly smile

At Man and all his avarice
His striving for 'the best'
Ignoring all the simple things
No time to sit and rest

Come sit my friend a little while
Come laugh and chat with me
Let's share a moment here on Earth
Beneath this old oak tree

Elizabeth Slater Hale

Time Well Spent

I smile each day,
Each dreary day
It helps to take the pain away
I laugh and joke my cares away,
For fear that they might always stay
I live each day as my last day,
It keeps those deadly blues at bay
I actively, positively work each day
So when He calls me I can say,
'I'm ready.'

Catherine Burtle

Revelations

When I awoke the sky was dim
and dark grey clouds were stamped
upon a sodden sky,
my mind sullen to the beat
of rain on the window,
unaware of the spiral coils
forming on the path below.

Heavy-eyed I glanced at a painting,
its tinsel colour gleamed
with shafts of emerald
floating in a sea of gold,
smudged cobalt shone like gems
in the mother-of-pearl frame.
That was when I became exhilarated
for the day had become
ruby-red shot with sapphire-blue.

Rosaleen Clarke

Inspired Reflections

Thoughtful and kind, so everlasting,
Oh thy God up in Heaven,
Who has great power over mankind,
God can no longer be denied by Man,

For He is the great triumphant King,
Women, those thoughtful creatures of mankind,
Who uplift Man's simple pleasures,
With the treasures of love and infinity.

Oh nature supreme with her simplicities,
With love and endearment, and beauty strong,
Like a guiding star in the vast heavens,
We have a lot to be thankful for,

While a child plays innocently in the secret garden,
Watched by beautiful women reflecting,
Reading rhyme, muse and poetry,
With spiritual dreams, the fairy queen has been,

To wave her magic wand of all she surveys,
The world and her blue magnificent oceans,
The trees, the mountains and the valleys below,
And all the scented aromatic flowers of the enchanted world.

Which we are able to smell, taste and touch,
Like a beautiful orchid and wild red wet rose,
Is to daydream alongside petal flowers upon your bed,
With their delicious dream perfumery,

Where the Roman god contemplates in glory,
With romantic nights beside the moonlit shore,
Apollo recites words of wisdom, love and hope,
Underneath the Mediterranean phantom sky,

Are spiritual beings ordained with love,
With a message of peace and thankfulness,
I wish I could be a follower of Jesus, and see the Bible is true,
I have admiration for your faith O Lord,

In the coming final days, to abide by the laws of God,
Who preacheth through His Son.

James Stephen Cameron

Untitled

Only a few weeks?
All my life have I known you.
Known you in the depth of my longing.
Known the faceless wonder of you.
Yet, only in the autumn of my life
Did I sight you,
When the light and warmth of summer
Had been crushed within me.
Then you came.
Came with the gentleness of an autumn breeze.
You came and you surrounded me
Softly, silently as the leaves fall.
You enveloped and you filled me
To overflowing
With a serenity of which I had not dreamed.
You filled me with strength to face the winter,
And hope . . . of another spring.

Petya Christie

Springtime Flowers

Hopefully as you read these words, they will somehow have a way,
of uplifting your spirit, bringing brightness to your day.
These words are written to remind you that the dark clouds in the sky,
never last forever and soon will pass you by.
Try to think of springtime flowers and the beauty they display,
and how they will survive the coldest winter's day.
Then as the sun shines in your eyes and the clouds have gently
passed, you will come to see, again you are shining brightly
in your soul, just like you used to be.

Karen Logan

That Special Ingredient

Like birth itself,
still a mystery,
unexpected and inescapable!
Challenging, potent,
and definitely part of us!
Ignored or cosseted,
trained or let loose!
The 'seeds' are accommodating
Responding as and when we choose,
dabbling or in earnest.
Fun, surprise, struggle
and inspiration go hand in hand,
hobbies or careers even
for us to choose
 - a wealth of talent
awaits to be discovered and explored
enriching every day.

Margaret Ann Wheatley

Believe In Your Heart

Believe in your heart that something wonderful is about to happen -
Love your life, believe in your powers and your own potential
And in your own innate goodness.
Wake every morning, with the awe of just being alive -
Discover each day the magnificent awesome beauty in the world.
Explore and embrace life - in yourself and in everyone you see!
Reach within, to find your own specialness; amaze yourself
And rouse those around you.
Don't be afraid to admit that you are less than perfect!
This is the essence of your humanity.
Let those who love you help you, trust enough to be able to take.
Look with hope to the new horizon of today -
For today is all that we truly have.
Live this day well - let a little sun out as well as in.
Create your own rainbows - be open to all your possibilities -
All possibilities and miracles - always believe in miracles.

Jacqui Allan

An Ode To Autumn

Autumn, your nature most gracious,
So fulsome like fruity red wine.
Your colours are all so vivacious
Golds, yellows, greens, reds, oh divine!
But you hold a secret behind gentle mirth,
As you cradle the land softly sighing,
While great is your beauty, you sing a swansong,
For in splendour you know you are dying.
So placing your children safe under the earth,
Awaiting spring to give them rebirth.
Happy now knowing that life will go on,
Turning on golden heels, swiftly you're gone.

Ann Slater

Sunday School And The Outing!

(For Miss Ivy Burnham of Bledlow Methodist Chapel)

Count your blessings, we sang,
As her nimble fingers ran across the old piano keys.
The yearly scripture exams behind us, we await the Whitsun service.
Our anniversary; our recitations learned
And musical duets for those with voices
To entertain the village, what a good job Ivy makes of those children!
At last the prizes given, and the certificates,
The great prize, a Bible inscribed with her small neat hand.

Jesus wanted us for His sunbeams, we were willing;
Waiting for the bull-nosed coach to take us off to Hayling Island
Little Hampton or Margate.
She in a crisp shirtwaister and neat sandals, a new hat for the outing,
We clutching new tin buckets and spades,
Thoughts of frothy, once a year, candyfloss, fish and chips for tea
Our mothers for once relaxing
Watching the endless journeys with buckets of salt water for our moats

We were all so H.A.P.P.Y. The sun always shining
Even the journey home, with an occasional try at Ten Green Bottles,
Was quiet now and drowsy,
Our only discomfort, the dusty moquette seats against our sunburn
We were safe in our little world, with Ivy.
Even now through cuttings with high chalk sides I still see her,
'This is the sort of place the Good Samaritan helped that poor man'
She said, leaving a picture for evermore imprinted in our minds.

Mary Anne Clock

A Recipe For Success

Ingredients:

Take a pinch of hope
Sprinkle it with optimism
Mix in three scoops of
sheer jammy good luck
(plain good fortune will do)
Add several kilos of hard work
(more may be needed as required)
One dollop each of
right place and right time
A measure of persistence
Stir with single-minded determination
Garnish with pleasure
Share with friends.

Method

If your dreams fail to come to fruition
And your hopes in tatters lie
Get back into the kitchen friend
Do not let those wishes die
It may take several batches
You might cook and bake and fry
Many times without results dear
But you must try and try and try.
Perhaps a different temperature
Or a change of baking tin
Make several minor adjustments
But never, ever give in
For that which is worth having
Does not come easily
If you feel you are not winning
Simply go back to the beginning.

Patricia Susan Dixon MacArthur

Leading The Lost To You

Lord, my heart it longs for You
But trembles deep inside
A thousand things I want to do
But often run and hide

I know that You have ransomed me
Paid with Your precious blood
Your living waters overflow
Saturating me with love

Jesus will You take my heart
And soften in Your hands
That I may take this wondrous news
And spread it through the land?

I know one day You'll call me home
And face to face we'll stand
With glistening jewels upon my head
I'll hold my daddy's hand

But in-between please help me Lord
Be bold, be strong and true
To stand, to fight and take the flack
And lead the lost to You

Allison Rynne

She Said Yes

You know I feel alive and I feel really great
To think it I could have lost
I could have been too late
But no, she said yes.

There I was all morning
Impatient, grooming madly to impress
A night of trepidation
All went when she said yes.

Last night I was lost on my bed in a catalogue of sad songs
Last night I dreamt I was a hero, righter of her wrongs
Last night I was sleepless thinking of her in my bed
That morning I went to ask her but I nearly turned away instead.

It was now or never, would I remember what to say?
The words I rehearsed all night, all morning
Would they desert me
Or at the crucial moment slip away?

I said it all so clumsily
If she did laugh, I'd run, I'd leave school
There is no refuge in the playground
For a mistaken, lovesick fool.

But it didn't matter, it took me by surprise
To find that I would be taking away the prize
But so quick a moment, did I hear her right?
Did she say yes and she would be happy
To walk with her home tonight?

Steve Prout

The Mirror

We change our life so many times
Day after day, time after time
We look in the mirror
We see the little child
Running in the field, running wild
We turn around again
The child has disappeared from the mirror
We see teenagers who are in love for the first time
So happy to be in love
So happy to be so young
We turn again and shocked I am
I see the little lady, I see the little man
With their grey hair and children all around
This is the granny, this is the grandad
The grandparents with big hearts
They change so many times in their lives
They change so many times.

M Motrici

Harmony

Sunshine and
Rain
In moderation
Speaks of a
World
Where emulation
Of a mastermind
Breathes an aura
Of universal
Regulation

L Merle Smith

My Ever-Faithful God

We are like ships in a tempestuous sea
Where waves and winds knock us constantly
But, it's His love that anchors me
My ever-faithful God

He is my rock and my very foundation
And His love and strength
Goes beyond all comprehension
And in Him is where I find my salvation
My ever-faithful God

Although at times, troubles may invade my days
I stand firm and it's His name I praise
And with joy and peace in my heart it says
My ever-faithful God

For after every storm comes a time of calm
And in His embrace He protects me from harm
With my name written on His palm
My ever-faithful God

Shirley Sewell

Untitled

I think if we can find
Success as bright as normal
In our dreams,
Then we can justly say
We are winning.
For the practical belies
The dreams of a god
With the hand of a man -
For we are gods somewhere else;
Here we are men in
The practical who cannot
Stop knowing eternity.

P T Barron

Love

Love is a word that means so much
Love is a word that you can't touch
Being in love with someone true
Loving someone just like you

Love is a word that tells you why
Love is a word that makes you cry
Being in love will make you see
That you and I were meant to be

Love is a word that passes by
Love is a word that gets you high
Being in love is all you need
Love will blossom like a seed

Love is a word that's always there
Love is a word for us to share
Being in love is made for two
Being in love is nothing new

Love is a word that cannot break
Love is a word that people take
Being in love will always stay
In your heart for every day.

Ryan Hepton

Floods

Across the water, and I'm missing you tonight,
Across the border, and I want to hold you tight,
To hold you in my arms,
To keep you safe and warm,
All I want to do is be with you.

Half a lifetime, and much more I'd wait for you,
Through the night-time, or across the ocean blue,
To catch you if you fall,
To answer if you call,
Wherever I may be, I'm here for you . . .

If we could reach a common ground,
Let floods and tears subside,
If we could build a bridge to bring -
Together you and I,
To cross that space between us,
To conquer that divide,
To feel each other's hearts beat close,
Together you and I,

Through the winter, and the cold of discontent,
I'd see the summer, if with you my days were spent,
To catch you if you fall,
To answer if you call,
In everything I do, I'm for you.

Paul Andrews

Poppies

Poppies.
By the side of the road,
Stuck in traffic.
The man in the car behind
Gets out and offers
A Quality Street!

Poppies.
A single poppy
In the field
My mum takes me,
To 'pick your own strawberries'
In the sun.

Poppies.
Along the tram tracks
As we round the corner.
On my way to date
The love of my life,
My future husband.

Poppies.
If you pick poppies,
The petals fall off.
I leave them growing
And grin with memories
Each time I pass by.

Lizzie Bailey

Galleries Of Our Minds

We all possess a gallery of our own,
Where unforgettable pictures can be stored.
And sometimes when we meditate alone,
The pictures from our galleries start to pour.

They may be scenes of glittering jewelled seas,
With shells strewn carelessly on creamy sands.
Or guided tours through lofty stately homes,
Where priceless treasures pose on moulded stands.

Once a knot of horses caught my eye,
Nodding graceful necks in harmony.
It seemed a conversation passed around,
Then on hind legs they reared, then turned to flee.

Another scene was chalets on a hill,
Where crimson flowers dripped from their balconies.
And in their gardens brilliant blues I saw,
As 'morning glory' cascaded from each tree.

One picture that's imprinted on my mind,
Is of a flower seller in a square.
With 'sweetpea', 'gyp' and 'roses' held aloft,
The sunlight caught her smile and soft grey hair.

My favourite picture from my gallery,
Is soft snow clinging close to grass and trees,
While carollers outside a cottage door,
Sang merrily, setting a perfect English scene.

Iris Forster

On The Other Side

From my troubled sleep,
A soft and gentle hand did creep,
It led me from my warm cocoon,
Outside shone the silvery moon.

Through the clouds we floated,
Left behind those on whom I doted,
Before us stood angels in white,
It was such a glorious sight.

Everyone was calm, at peace,
Surrounded by clouds of fleece,
Harps played melodies sweet,
Everyone went round with bare feet.

An angel took me by the hand,
It's time to return to your land,
For you it's not time to stay,
We will meet again another day.

My eyes opened wide,
Had I been on the other side?
Rested and trouble-free I felt,
Another chance at life I was dealt.

Carol Paxton

Fate

You could be an angel sitting on a park bench,
You could be a stranger stranded on a mountain ledge,
You could be parading along golden sandy shores,
You could be on a boat floating without oars,
You could be in a cage at the bottom of the sea,
You could have walked past not noticing me,
You could be in the dreams I cannot remember,
You could be where the rainbow ends asleep in treasure,
You could have lived in the past or be born in the future,
You could be on another planet or in Heaven forever,
You could be the spirit that coexists within me,
You could be in the mirror but I cannot see,
You could be thinking of me thinking of you,
You could hear me calling out aloud too,
Whoever you are and wherever you may be,
One day fate will bring you to me.

Aron M Robinson

So Let's Go

So let's go
Climb a mountain
Like we used to
Just because we could
Just because it was there

So let's go
Face that challenge
Like we used to
Just because we could
Just because it was there

So let's go
And slip this safe harbour
Before age defeats our will
Just because we still can
Just because we think we're young

Come on, come on
We should be going
Come on, come on
We should be leaving
Come on, come on
We should be gone

R R Gould

The Jewel In The Crown

Now, we see through a glass darkly, but then we shall know,
                         as even also we are known.

Who are we? How seldom do we pause awhile and contemplate
                         the wonder of our being?
Man to the moon must go and sate his curiosity, it is inevitable.
But the uncharted depths of his own personhood remain a mystery,
A journey too hazardous to contemplate, unfathomable, our history.

Will he be too lost in the jungle, and fail to untangle
                    and unravel the maze,
As he contemplates his own complexity,
But should he persevere, he will find the jewel in the crown,
The very heart of the universe, which throbs with every breath we take,
Christ in him, the hope of glory,
What an epic wonder, what a story!

That the Creator of the universe, the three in one, should deign
                    to abide in us, and we in Him,
Lifts our whole personhood into realms of the divine
If in this world only we have hope, we are of men most miserable,
But no, eternity, infinity, is planned to be our destiny.
Our sights fixed on the race, the cross, the crown,
Overcoming all which pulls us down,
Revelling in the strength within.
Resting, yea, nestling in them, in Him.

Beryl Moorehead

A Vision

The walls speak to you,
Lined with verse and song,
A vision of God's creation,
For today if one word brings comfort,
Tomorrow might bring joy,
And the next a spiritual cleansing,
For season upon season the void will be filled,
Each step to 'The Upper Room' a journey,
Vibrant and colourful the inner beauty glows,
The mind is fed and the soul will grow,
God's light shining through the darkness,
Unfolding into untold beauty.

'For God be the glory,
Great things He has done'.

Nadine Mackie

Silver Lining

Don't you know every cloud has a silver lining?
Don't you see the sun above you keep on shining?
The world above you wants you to start new
Don't you see the sky above is a sparkly blue?
You should have known that your life would get better
Didn't you realise what was in that letter?

Your life is forever beautiful and so it will carry on
Your life will remain to be beautiful even after you've gone
Live each day like it will be your last
Get out there and start having a blast
Your life is special, don't ever feel it's not
Don't you ever think it's tied in a knot

Don't ever stand for people wanting to judge you
You shouldn't let them do that, should you?
I don't think people should act this way
I don't think people should put up with this every single day

Kylie Mills

Mercy

God of the unexpected,
prompting the inner thought to pray
that moment of empathy
over a news item, far away.

God of the dare to dreamtime,
the doors that appear to close
that revelation of hope
above flustered throes.

God of the resolution
found in a divided world
the turning of the other cheek,
the voice of a child.

God of the widow's mite
the trust in giving
the unobserved, unnoticed
talent that gives life to the living.

Naomi Lange

Me

I look in my mirror, what do I see?
A reflection looking back at me.
Who am I? I cannot recall
Alzheimer's has taken its toll.
I want my mum and my dad,
a stranger tells me they are long gone.
I pace for hours, my work is never done,
the babies are crying, where are they now?
Two men sit across from me,
they say they are my sons,
I don't know these persons, where can I run?
I look a little closer, one of them looks a bit like me,
I give him a smile, he holds out his hand.
I touch it politely, it seems enough -
I settle more comfortably, so does he.
A glimmer of hope resides within me.

Glenda Barker

I Am So Lucky

I count my blessings, every day,
and to God, I often pray,
to keep me well; to carry on,
as I am a widow, and live alone.

When I look around and see some folk
in wheelchairs; who cannot walk,
I feel so lucky, that I am not chairbound,
and that I am privileged to be able to get around.

Mary Crickmore

Time To Wonder!

From near to far,
Through this land,
Of beauty where miracles are,
Time to wonder,
These lands that are so pure,
Wonder through the woodlands,
And by the riversides also hills,
Which may be new to my eyes,
Time to wonder where the sun shines
All of the day,
Yes God has blessed me,
With such a miracle,
In so many ways.

C Hush

Maria Makiling

Her name tinkles, like dancing bamboo,
Like quick maya birds darting, chattering,
Like leaping, skittering deer and faun
On rich deep-leaved forest floor.
She drinks with the animals from running streams,
Cups clear water in her hands, pulls wild fruit
From hanging boughs, harms not the beasts.
Take a while under the tallest trees,
Breathe in deep, raise your arms high
Palms up like growing sapling, and you will feel
Her presence, joyous, benign, like slanting sun.
She is the spirit of great mountains,
A lithe and primeval being; long before
Stone and clay were raised into walls,
Palm leaves heaped into shelter,
Fire harnessed into heat and light
And barriers grew around our lives,
She moved, laughing, strong and free
Amongst the birds and deer, her wild face
Dappled with gold, light catching
On high cheekbones, glinting in hazel eyes,
Long hair swaying curved as tree snake,
Long legs dancing, bare feet pure.
And still she wafts alone in morning mist,
Still people arrive late, despite the armour
Of roaring, adorous modern cars,
On frantic roads like metal scars,
Breathless and awed, they gape,
Entranced by her magical form;
Swear blind they see her, drifting across
Roads and paths with her animals close,
Maria Makiling, woodland spirit.
They try to capture her in concrete,
Lumpen and gauche; idealised on canvas,
Wide-eyed, glossy and glam, but no,
She shines and darts like sun on wet leaves,
Cannot be caught, like quicksilver,
Maria Makiling, tinikling, tinikling . . .

Liz Davies

Hope

There's a purpose for my living
And a reason I was born.
I delight my heavenly Father,
His love for me is sworn.

I have a hope eternal:
This flame will never die.
I have a home with Jesus,
The apple of my eye.

I live to bring Christ glory
In all I do and say.
For such a time as this
Was why I was made this way.

No matter how dark the night gets
Or how I feel inside
I know that God's love stays firm:
He'll claim a conquering bride.

Ruth M Ellett

Comforting Carpet

Beautiful bluebells -
Providing pieces of
Comforting carpet for
Lost, low lambs in
Dells not dales.

Azure plus aroma.
Wafting in wind quite
Freely - each friend -
Nodding nonchalantly
Amongst blue
After blue, after blue -
Piece of peace.

Jac C Simmons

The Last Of The Sunshine

Beauty on a gaze,
upon the first, the last and always look,
love is the word that a mouth reaches for,
soulful smile and a lifetime of happiness.
To know her is to have known pure splendour,
true pleasure for a world so bare.
A mind so intense,
there's nowhere to look but for deep inside,
looking for the most elaborate of answers.
Searching for what her heart desires but it is staring at her,
with woeful eyes and a childish smile,
their destinies forever entwined.
She is hidden,
every part of her being is trapped by the chains of life,
the things others must follow,
must obey,
the rules.
Breaking free in a life no one can prepare for,
ready for anything that may challenge her,
stop her on her path,
she is always ready.
Determination running through her veins like blood,
her life source.
Passionate about her dreams,
hoping to succeed.
An ambition to see into the unknown,
the darkness,
we have yet to explore.
An understanding of all things,
yet she asks for nothing in return.
When you see her,
standing,
fighting,
all of it to save us,
you will not only see the woman she is but was.
The woman who not only saved the world but helped to create it.
Each passing moment and time stands still,
the world waits on bated breath,
for an entrance of anticipation,

as she walks into the room,
all eyes fallen on the innocence of perfection,
in its true form,
untouched by all but God's own hands.
Through eyes of mystery,
we see darkness behind us,
the light guiding through the shadows,
from the warmth of her heart
and the deepness of her soul.
We follow in admiration,
we follow in belief,
we follow her because,
we know she is there for our protection.
We know she will fall,
we will all fall as well,
hitting hard the earth
as we lose sight of her innocence
and set out to once again search
the forbidden and unknown.
Frightened by ourselves,
scared to be alone,
fearing the darkness without her.
Terrified of the light,
without protection,
a warm and loving hand to guide us through.
We need her to be the one who is our sunshine
through the times of shadows.
She will be
the moment
in which a life will be lived.
When someone will fulfil their dreams
because they needed her to heed their call and help them prevail.
With her eyes still shining and full of friendship,
she lays a smile upon our lips and a thought in our mind,
a hole filled where once there was nothing but the cold
                                                    of the midnight sky.
Shaking during the coldness of her plight to freedom,
we acknowledge it but wish she would return,
                                we are useless without her,
we feel lost but the world feels vulnerable,
enough for them to fall apart.

Broken pieces of lives, lay a mound on the earth.
Will the fallen spirit in which she had been entrusted within,
be within our hearts once again?
To rid the world of its evil
and rid our hearts of the despair it had once
been seduced by.

To free us from our chains and make us happy once again,
from the first moment we saw her,
to the last moment we close our eyes, we feel the love
                        she shines and the comfort of her smile.
To give us hope once again, as it is she who spreads it
                                        within our hearts.

Donna Mapals

The Winner Is . . .

Buy one get one free.
Today's jargon for
A shopping spree.
Household goods
And wearing apparel.
Necessary, of course.

But spare a moment -
Your well-trimmed lawn
Be it large or small,
Will never hide the daisy.
Do they still make the daisy chains for neck or waist?
A pity modern inventions take over.
But for how long?
The daisies are with us
Forever and free.
Thank God.

Isobel Scarlett

Silvery Blue

Wreathing, writhing and curling like a snake,
The silvery blue mist came down by the lake:
Creeping up over the houses and barns:
Heard - but not seen - the tinkling tarns.

The earth was trying hard to wriggle through
The long, wreathing, misty, silvery blue;
Yet - way up above - the heavens were clear,
The sun was shining bright up there, so near.

But Mother Nature, she had on her shroud;
This mistiness was not a passing cloud,
The clinging mist clung to the shrubs and trees:
Hiding in foliage were birds and bees.

Suddenly, the struggling sun it broke through,
And all the flowers were covered in dew:
The swirling mist rolled away into space;
Nature put on again a smiling face!

J Millington

A Certain Kind Of Beauty

There's a certain kind of beauty
In the small face of a child
A certain kind of innocence
That comes with every smile

There's a certain kind of beauty
In those eager, shining eyes
That sparkles even brighter
With each successful thing he tries

There's a certain kind of beauty
That passes each child's lips
As the questions, all the whys and hows
Seeking knowledge he can grip

There's a certain kind of beauty
In those small and delicate hands
Ever trying to touch each little thing
Until he knows and understands

There's a certain kind of beauty
In each and every child
And you'll see it every time you look
Into a child's smile

Victorine Lejeune Stubbs

In My Solitude

In my solitude
I find
The peace of God
In my solitude
I find the stillness
The gentleness
Of the Holy Spirit.
In my solitude
I feel His presence
So very near.
It is in my solitude
I feel His strength.
For He answers me
In God's time.
For He is God Almighty
The amaziness of God.
He comes with healing.
So beautiful in the quietness
He knows He hears.
For God is God.
He knows all that is within.
I only have to sit
In my solitude
The peace of God
That passeth
All Man's understanding.

Maureen Thornton

Just A Thought Away

There's a little cottage in the country,
just waiting for me.
It's in the land of golden dreams,
right beside the sea.
The wildflower garden is Heaven's scent,
and surrounds me with peace,
and a shady quiet spot awaits
underneath the trees.
There are roses round the door frame,
nesting birds nearby,
and pure white fluffy clouds,
in a clear blue sky.
The sound of a trickling water pool,
is a melody so fair,
and whenever I need that special place,
my mind transports me there.

P Hardman

Solace In Friends

Our earthly journey,
Brings us many experiences 'twixt joy and grief,
Along the route we encounter many unexpected obstacles,
That we need to surmount,
To enable us to move on to yet another day,

Through faith we seek the fortitude,
To see the trials through to conclusion,
Family rally around us to bring comfort and support,
Partners bring us the stability and love,
That we need at this juncture,

Yet it's at these times of extreme vulnerability,
That our true friends come shining through,
Cradling us in a cocoon of compassion,
Offering sincere words and assistance,
With them we can be ourselves to the point of truth,

We all live at a hectic pace,
With not much time for relaxation,
Expectations of our lifestyle are much higher,
In this materialistic age,
We become fraught with anxiety and stress,

Advances in science and technology constantly change,
Broadening horizons in an ever-changing world,
Yet we all need friends,
A warm smile and a welcome face,
Someone who listens and genuinely cares,

Those who know our foibles and inner fears,
Cheer us up, and in doing so carry a part of our burden,
They are the cushions amongst the rocks,
On which to lay our heads awhile,
In these, our friends, we can take solace.

Ann G Wallace

Inner Strength

My attitude to all of life
Has changed in recent years:
Since I became a pensioner
I've lost so many fears.

No more taking things for granted;
I've found a hidden voice,
Which tells me to express myself
And firmly state my choice.

I can't believe its taken me
So long to be so 'cool';
But, since I've found such freedom,
I won't be made the fool.

Having gained this self-willed power,
I'll give it of my best.
My free and new-found spirit
Will pass the toughest test.

Brian M Wood

Sun Spiders

The outside of the window
was covered with broken rainbows;
the gossamer of spiders' webs.
Morning sun had transformed it
into a thing of beauty.
Not just for looking through
or another thing to clean.

As I shut my mind to time
and slowly turned around my head,
threads of colours joined together.
Gloriously dispersed then rejoined.
Magenta, heavenly blue,
orange, green, and yellow
of a thousand daffodils.

The rainbows reminded me of God's promise.

Pearl Foy

Encouragement

The hurly-burly of modern life,
Stuck on the road in a traffic jam;
The train's late again, snow on the line,
Will I ever get to work on time?

Just close your eyes and drift away,
Lie on the beach, take in the sun;
Waves lap at your feet, float away
In a silent world of your own.

Winter is here, snow's on the way,
The storm's just blown your fencing down;
Dark clouds of black, drab skies of grey,
Chill winds force you to wear a frown.

Think of the joys that come with spring;
Buds on the branch burst into green,
Sweet birdsong and tunes fill the air,
Pink and white blossom stand serene.

The cold north wind blows on your coat,
Trudging on, you feel so tired,
Think of how soon you will be home,
The roaring flicker of the fire.

Think of those who don't have a home;
A garden bench or just a squat,
A disused shed or old warehouse
Or a hostel could be their lot.

Think of the pleasure of giving:
Sad faces starting to shine;
Think of the pleasure of living:
Making 'ours' out of 'mine'.

Anne Lever

Don't Despair

Don't despair,
From out of the blue,
A solution will come to mind,
In the cold light of day,
You will surely find,
Cares that weigh heavy,
Will lighten, from the bind,
Of a conscience of frailty,
Of a nether kind.

Don't despair,
Delve into subconscious,
Let thought waves flow,
Stay single-minded,
Then somehow you'll know,
The problem when courted,
Even when you feel low,
Will eventually be righted,
And dispel threat of woe.

Don't despair,
Take courage from a clear head,
Face the torment, don't wilt,
Problems are solvable,
When hopes have been built,
Success doesn't come easy,
Clear your heart of any guilt,
Go forward with determination,
Use guile up to the hilt.

Don't despair,
The time will surely come,
When worry will leave your heart,
No more will the turmoil,
Forever tear you apart,
The easiness in mind,
Clearing mists for a start,
Conquering your fears,
Making them depart.

William G Stannard

Miracles And Wonders

Early one morning, just as the sun was rising
It was not a maiden calling
That greeted my blessed ears
But birds in their almighty throng
Simultaneously bursting into song
Greeting the dawn with their sweet, melodic cheers

It was not three ships a-sailing by
I saw on Christmas morning
But a shooting star above me fly
While I was still yawning

It was not a crop circle so mysterious
That made me stare at the field
Nor was it the thought of how much would be made
In money from its yield
It was the way the sun danced upon it
The way the breeze whispered through it
Its beautiful, golden hue
It was alive, glorious and new

It was not of Noah and his ark I thought
When all those animals home I brought
Nor were they a new kind of toy
I had just opened my heart to them
And they filled it up with joy

You don't need a Bible or spiritual quest
A sweat lodge or a special test
Or to travel away so far
Miracles and wonders are who and where you are
They are in a single snowdrop
They are the scent of a garden rose
They are that butterfly so perfect
They *are* that baby's toes
They are beneath you on the ground you tread
They are above you in the skies
To experience miracles and wonders
You have naught to do, but open your eyes.

L Hughes

Becoming

Unbeknown to me she had hidden in my home,
in some tight dark chink between furniture,
had squeezed her fat body wrapped in its
fur coat that now showed, and bore traces
of dust that she had not yet combed out
and brushed off. The coloured bands around
her abdominal bulge were dulled by dust.

Now she climbed up my window curtain,
making all kinds of fuss, I could see that she
still had not fully woken up, she grumbled,
talking to herself in exasperated intermittent,
irritated buzzes and hums - but gradually,
warmed by the sun, her tiny but powerful
engines came on-song - began to run.

Unhurriedly she cleans herself of all traces
of her long sleep, the dust combed out she
cleans her legs and each pair of wings -
freshened up, she powers up - revs up
wing beats, then nose up close to stall,
she lifts off, and for the first time
in five months, she flies.

I watch, and at the right moment
open my window wide and let her rise
head out and up, into the clear blue
waiting sky - see her become a shrinking
small black dot - making a beeline for the sun.
The search for her summer palace,
her royal nursery has begun.

Rick Storey

Sunshine After Rain

When adversity strikes I find,
A prayer gives me peace of mind.
I pray for the strength to carry on,
And my troubles will soon be gone.

God has never let me down so far,
He's always been my guiding star.
Sometimes I pray far into the night,
Asking for His help to make things right.

We do not know what the future holds,
Only hope for the best as life unfolds.
A mixture of good events and bad,
Experiences veer from happy to sad.

In the stormy whirlpool of life,
There is often discord and strife.
But it is just passing through,
Soon the dark clouds fade from view.

Remember God is always there,
So our problems we can share.
We will learn to smile again,
Just like the sunshine after rain.

Rosemary Davies

Wealthier Families

Above and beyond the perils of Earth
Far and away from the rich and obscene,
Are wealthier families of wisdom and girth
Holding the torch and loving supreme.
Collectively driven they watch and observe
Always on hand to capture the soul,
They preside over time and always preserve
The beautiful hearts of the young and the old.
Never growing weary of showing the way
With no puffed up egos or war hungry wills,
They don't use a voice but have plenty to say
The gifts that they hold are a licence to thrill.
No secret codes open doors to their world
The password is written all over your heart,
Your soul is a canvas encrusted with pearls
Caressing the brushstrokes of celestial art.

Andrew Hobbs

Thought

A
Thought
Approaches
Like a
Person
Aiming to
Tap someone
Upon the
Shoulder,
Pausing,
Forgetting,
Thinking to itself,
Hovering,
Dithering,
Unavailable
As silence,
Sleep or
Distant
Noises.

Nicola Barnes

Clouds

When clouds hang low upon your life
And scenes around are dismal, dark and grey,
Can you hear the sparrows singing in the trees
And understand the message they convey?

Their melody is sounding near and far -
A happy song we all do well to heed,
For they're not dismayed by dismal signs around
They know their every need is supplied indeed.

For the One who cares for sparrows cares for us
We're included in the embrace of His love,
So amidst life's clouds let's raise a heartfelt song
In thanksgiving to the God who reigns above.

Stanley Birch

Worry

Why do we worry? Why do we care?
Our feelings we will not share
But what is the point of keeping it inside
When really there is nothing to hide?

Why worry for the future you cannot see?
For when it comes it will 'have to be'
What a relief when things turn out fine
And you say how silly, I've been out of my mind

Remember today and not tomorrow
The time we have got is only borrowed

Pat Jakes

The Foxglove

My being is neither wild nor tame,
For I am the lyrics whispering in the rain
For I am the keyboard strum by the breeze,
I am the one, who heals heart's disease.

I disrobe slowly
My petals falling on to the dewy grass
Yet I know, this is all a farce.
Angels come to bathe here,
While fairies sip their tea.

I never die!
I merely recline
And begin on next year's
Symphony.

Luci Sale

God Bless

With my prayer I lit a candle
Hoping wishes could come true.
I watched the holy light flickering
As my prayer winged its way to You.
I prayed again in thankfulness
For blessings that came my way.
In fact there were a thousand prayers
For there were blessings each day.
I often prayed for an answer
And an answer would always come.
How often You led me from the darkness
Into the warmth of the sun.
I want to say thank You . . .
Although thank You is inadequate I guess
So I can only say that I truly know
The meaning of those words . . . God bless.

Joyce Hudspith

Support

(Based on Exodus 17:12)

Dear Lord and Father,
When sometimes the battle of life
Becomes too much for me,
Remind me that all I need do
Is to lift my hands in prayer to You.
If even then my prayers start faltering,
Let me call on the strength of my friends
To support my prayers through the day.
For the infinite blessing of prayer,
Dear Lord and Father
I thank You.

Di Bagshawe

Bow My Rain

How can hearts be pained and dry
yet through your presence lift the sky,
and with your deliverance,
make me cry?

Why is happiness like a knife
severing limbs and cold as ice,
yet with your outline
save my life?

Is there an end to twisted fate
perhaps with the making of a date,
and with your promise,
my pain sedate?

So train your way to me again
unlock your heart's refrain
and with your journey . . .
bow my rain.

Andrew Bott

Sweet Mother Of Mine

You used to nurse me on your knee
And sing sweet lullabies to me.
I loved to brush your hair of gold.
You were a picture to behold.

I kissed away your fears and tears.
You've grown more precious through the years.
And though your hair has turned to grey
I love you more and more each day.

Helen Barwood

Fireworks

Fireworks erupting very bright
Fireworks lighting up the night
Colours exploding in the sky
Everyone gazing with a satisfied eye
Catherine wheels spinning near the ground
It makes you dizzy watching them go round and round
Rockets starting off on the grass
Zoom into the sky
Making everyone gasp
As they go by.

Charlotte Adams (9)

Home And Garden

My little home so welcoming, is where
I lay my head. The place where I can be
Myself. My chair, that dear old sofa bed . . .
Where I can stretch, relax, take time, be me.

And just beyond the window, the garden
Waits for me; to tend the plants, cut the grass.
Then watch as nature holds my gaze, the jargon
As the birds will nest. The flowers that last . . .

Year in and on to procreate with Sun:
Rain to feed; push life on. The changing face
Of nature in itself, so all at one
In tranquillity, beauty, peace and grace.

No other place on Earth could ever bring
Such joy and inner pleasure, make me sing.

Pearl M Burdock

Gentle Thoughts

The green leaves of summer
Sway on gentle breeze;
Birdsong heralds the season
Of golden sunshine
         And azure skies:
Across the landscape
         Leaping time beckons
The weary traveller
         Towards the ringing bells.
Seasons pass,
         But still men dream.

Arthur Pickles

He's With The Angels Now

(Bryn Cory Gulley)

It broke your parents' heart in two
The day they had to part with you
For nothing could prepare them for
A life without their baby boy.

With blanket swathed around you tight
They kissed and held you really tight
They knew you'd never meet again
Which made them really writhe in pain,

Now every year that passes by
You're missed so much your parents cry
The only comfort they have found
Is knowing God is with you now.

So . . . every time you go to sleep
Your parents hope the angels keep
A watchful eye on you dear Bryn
Because you meant so much to them.

But since the day you passed away
A little daughter came their way
Perhaps it was a gift from God
To make up for the son they lost.

Merilyn E A Gulley

Lilian

Lovely Lily pure and fair
On her shoulders not a care
Up and down the room she trips
Laughter bubbles from her lips
Tiny teeth like shiny pearls
Rosy cheeks and golden curls
Dressed in white and blue and pink
What a diva, don't you think?
Take a picture, snap it fast
Treasured moments made to last.

Muriel Nicola Waldt

Let's Get Together

(A Black Forest meditation)

After a day in a coach enclosed
We glimpsed a magical diorama
Even though tired, not well-disposed
We viewed a sumptuous panorama.
A village church, lean-steepled there,
Clustered by steep-roofed dwellings,
Green, rising, lush grass meadows fair
Capped by forest land up swelling.
The prelude to a time at rest
In village inn all snug and homely,
With English, Dutch and German guests
All gathered there so prim and comely.
At dinner on the opening night
We stayed all in our proper places.
All sitting, chatting, holding tight,
Each in respective races.
Scheduled to fill a later gap,
Behold! A folk night celebration,
With glorious 'oompah' band on tap
Fuelled marvellous expectation.
'Laugh and be happy' so they say,
Count blessings, have some fun.
We soon felt in a special way
Friendships at last begun.
The evening passed with great acclaim,
With many joint gyrations,
And, at the end, we all became
A wondrous league of nations.

Jack Scrafton

I Have A Friend In Jesus

I have a friend in Jesus
I do not walk alone
He is the only one
All I ever want is just to be with Him.
He is the only One, the One, and only One,
No one else can fill my life the way He does.
My soul He satisfies
In sorrow, He's my comfort.
He gives me a song in the night
He dries my tears and drives away my fears.
In my darkest hours I feel His gentle touch
And hear His still-small voice within my soul.
That voice I hear so clearly, so softly.
I know it is not my voice nor my own words I hear.
He is the great 'I am'.
You ask me how I know He lives?
I feel Him in my soul!
If healing I need, I hear that still-small voice saying,
'I am going to heal you'.
In sorrow I feel His warm embrace,
The glory of His presence all around me brightening up my way.
Then I hear Him say, 'Trust My todays, trust My tomorrows,
I hold the future!'
Oh, then I know, they are not my todays,
They are not my tomorrows, they are His.
So why should I worry when He is in control.
He's my best friend and He will see me through for He has said,
'I will never leave you, nor forsake you'.

Joy Wilson

Promised Land

Oh bright sunshine that hath been
my guiding light throughout my years,
wouldst thou within these days serene,
hide thyself behind the clouds? Fears

that pursue me in this hallowed life,
that now turns to darkness before my eyes,
and wing-ed angels in my hour of strife
spread their wings before me as life dies.

And now I stand afore those gates
that yield with but one trembling hand.
Where evil thoughts there dissipates
and hence I reach my Promised Land.

Brian Richard Bates

Easter Joy

An empty tomb - new life, new hope
Rejoice with every breath
Our sins have been forgiven and
The Lord has conquered death

Today the world has been released
From fear of death's dark prison
For Jesus, who was crucified
Still lives - the Lord is risen!

So no more gloom, despair or doubt
Be filled with faith and joy
We have a living Saviour's love
Which *nothing* can destroy

Helen M Clarke

Meeting In Prayer

Thoughts and feelings
Connect us,
Wherever and whenever,
For
Shortened is the distance,
And
Lessened is the time,
For our hearts
And minds
To meet in prayer!

Cornelius Mulvaney

Beautiful Things

It's good to see the sunset
All thoughts, hopeful and true
It's amazing
What love can do

Who can paint the sky
Like Hockney and Van Gogh?
Who can sing a song
Like Tom Jones and Rod Stewart?

It's things like this that cheer me up
When I've got a bad throat
And a blocked-up nose
Life is good in you

Kenneth Mood

Revelling

Put it all away to come with me along the path of revelry
To make the leapfrog leap to lily leaf, and suck the passionflower
                                    and darkly deep
Make, in the brushwood and the ferns, a flowing bower of gauzy moss
To sleep and sleep upon an unencumbered hour, fast lost
Put it all away
and dreaming past the broken stones, enchantment find in mended
                        bones and soothing sips and lily tips

Put away the soaring sordid song, the prong of broken heart from
                                    now on
Don't take it back and come away with the hurting from the
                                hurting brave
The joyless twitch, the grisly shower, the missing laugh that once
                                    was ours

Put it all away and come revel in the mimicry
And if you don't come again, to tilt the pansy of the brain
In shadowy places of the mind and velvet toss
The strain and speckled silver streak of starlit night, and wonders meet
I'll come and revel in the loss, in the path that once was crossed
Then put it all away.

R A Toy

The Blackbird Song

A peacock butterfly flitters its wings
On the garden shed a blackbird sings
A muntjac visits the bubbling brook
Overhead cry a multitude of rooks

Bumblebees flitter from flower to flower
Blackbird sings hour after hour
A spotted woodpecker lands on a log
Across the lawn hops a green frog

Then a horse walks across the yard to the stable
Collared doves arrive at the bird table
Sunlight sparkles on the pond
Still the blackbird sings along

A trio of ducks leave their safe retreat
Blackbird decides to change the beat
Squirrels leap from branch to branch
Ants emerge and decide to march

Blackbird's melody has filled the air
Hour after hour he has been sitting there
On the shed he has spent the day
Singing his heart out
Now he has flown away

Christine Hardemon

Human Curiosity

Stare at the stars
Wondering
Which one is Mars,
Face in the moon
Remind me of whom?
Group of stars
That make up the big bear,
Twinkling up there.
Where are the guiding hands
That guide the plough?
Will these invisible hands
Human curiosity hide?
Will it be common
For starships
To fly by?
Clouding over,
All my starry wonders
Drift behind the clouds,
No clouds
Shroud
My wonders.

Bryan Clarke

The Recalcitrant Dieter

Oh! Woeful day that doctors should
Declare fat bad and thinness good!
I don't outgrow my clothes, you know -
The damp, dank wardrobe shrinks them so!

The scales we scan with bated breath -
Too many pounds count us to death -
But many to the crem will go
Whose calorie intake was low.

So - who'll enjoy their pot of cream?
'Anoint my pud!' I hear you scream.
One must have sugar on the berry -
And if a short life, then merry.

If all were thin, we'd live too long.
The weak are sickly - some are strong.
We don't know when or why we go -
But many do whose weight was low!

Jacqueline Morris

A Quantum Leap (By An Open Window)

(A moment in time)

Breezes lift curtains
To billow and sway,
A bee at the window
Buzzes away,
Warm summer air
Caresses the day.

Everything stills to the
Inward eye, a weightless
Existence of colour and sky,
An integral part of the
Beat of a heart.

Life in its fullness
A parallel dream,
All of it purpose
There to redeem:
Time suspended in
A perfect design,
All of its wisdom
Suddenly mine.
The answers were here
Like a sacred scroll,
The light of eternity
Touching my soul.

A flutter of wings,
A blackbird in song
Perceived as an anthem
That must be prolonged.

A distant door slams,
A shadow is cast,
A breath of anguish
As the moment is lost.

Colleen Biggins

A Question Of Faith

If you believe
With all your might,
In mind, body and soul,
You might find
Just what you're looking for.
Don't ask why
Cos it's a question of faith.
But you've got to search
For where Heaven on Earth is,
Who the perfect soulmate is,
What the best things in life are,

Which hidden qualities there are,
When to aim for the ultimate,
How to make dreams come true.
You've got to go on searching
Until all corners of the world are explored,

That special someone is found,
The essence of life is discovered.
All inner strengths are revealed,
All limits are transcended,
Then a life of fantasies can be lived.
You mustn't give up
Hope mustn't falter,
Fears must be alleviated,
Success is paramount,
Failure isn't an option,
Otherwise,
Faith is ridiculed.

Eunice Ogunkoya

Happy Of Heart

Be happy of heart
let your spirit be light
through the sun and rain,
the day and the night.
Greet each morn with a smile,
each dusk with a little pleasure
and for the waking while,
life will be your treasure!

Andrew Gruberski

The World Wasn't Made Just For You

It's time to change
To change our ways
To open our eyes as well as new doors
To open our hearts, to not even scores
Our throwaway outlook builds mounds of waste
Our conveyor-belt ideals to please all tastes
Alarm clocks sound, the dangers are real
We think we cannot be hurt
By things out of view
It's time to change
The world wasn't made just for you
We don't need or want half of what is on the shelves
So who's kidding who?
Supermarket managers
Or are we just kidding ourselves?

Mike Hynde

Lonely, But Not Solely

The weather is wet and cold,
Not a pleasure when you are old
And living on your own,
Interests needed to atone.

What might those interests be?
Let's take a look and see,
Being forced to stay indoors
There are, of course, household chores.

The latter not likely your spirit raise,
Perhaps a bottle might bring praise,
For some TV could be enough,
Or maybe something a bit more tough.

The elderly, exercise is often too much,
They could be rewarded with a touch,
Music too does ease your mind,
Suitable sources not difficult to find.

Some might prefer to read,
While women knit to succeed,
Others on canvas like to paint,
Arts and crafts, some quite quaint.

Writing poetry might fill the book,
Prose too is there to hook,
Many ways to ease the strain,
Without over-taxing that old brain.

But company is the real treat,
Pleasant conversation you cannot beat,
With others exchange comment,
Surely this will bring content.

George Beckford

Hope

The rain beats heavily against the windowpane
The sky is black and clouds obscure the way,
The wind is howling above the rooftop
As I wake to face another day.
I throw aside the quilted cover
And glance through the wet patterns on the glass.
In the distance the sky glows red at daybreak
And I know a new day dawns, yesterday is past.
I cannot live in its history
I move on to live and build new dreams,
As the sun breaks through the darkened skyline
And I awake to new challenges, new plans, new schemes.
Without the dark clouds, I could not appreciate the sunlight
Without the rain, the sun offers only dry, parched ground,
In the stillness of the morning
I appreciate each new sound.
I cannot know the rich experience that only sorrow brings,
I could never soar to heights unknown
And know the freedom borne on wings.
Shadows are only shadows cast by a bright and shining light
Oh the joy and strength of sunrise
Dispelling the darkness of the night.

Maralyn Molyneux

Blessings In Unexpected Places

For me,
Blessings appear in unexpected places,
Amongst the depths of despair
Where surely they cannot survive.
Amongst the uncertain future of my illness
And yet they appear, on the face of a loved one,
The visit of a friend, the card and the flowers
Which lift me up in renewed hope.

For me,
Blessings appear in unexpected places
And bring a new sharpness to my world.
A fallen leaf, a sparrow feeding,
The sunrise marking a new dawn
Amongst the uncertain future of my illness
And I treasure those precious moments of my life
Which lift me up in renewed hope.

For me,
Blessings appear in unexpected places
When the dark moments cast their shadows.
And the treatment brings fatigue
And a sense of despair
And then the love and comfort of those close to me,
The visit of a friend, the card and the flowers
Lift me up in renewed hope

And I count my blessings.

Maurice Turner

Life's Beautiful Things

When life feels too heavy to just shrug it off -
when you're down and alone with your thoughts.
When no one's around and you're feeling so lost -
try to remember the lessons life's taught.

Just take your time - let yourself relax -
no feelings of guilt or shame.
Be kind and gentle to yourself then perhaps
you'll feel stronger to re-enter life's games.

You are the stranger whom I clearly recognise -
exhausted from the wraths of time!
Feeling you simply want to close your eyes -
far too tired to even cry!

Just remember, tho' we are strangers -
that when you take a closer look -
there's a tiny piece of each of us
within the pages of this book!

And together - tho' we are strangers -
a part of each one makes a whole.
So be brave - take your time - then continue
on the pathway towards your goals!

Visualise some of life's beautiful things -
colourful butterflies - birds on the wing!
The robin that watches as you mow the lawn -
the heavenly chorus that wakes us at dawn!

The songthrush - the ladybird - the dragonflies -
blackbird is pulling up worms.
The cotton-wool clouds way up in the sky -
a safe ceiling for us here on Earth!

As you lay your head down on the pillow
may God's angels smooth away your cares.
May you dream the sweetest dreams - of pretty fairy scenes -
and may God listen - very closely - to your prayers!

Tomboy

Autumn's Symphony

A time of peace
When Mother Nature prepares
For the winter's chill -
She paints the colours of the Fall
Upon the horizons of time.

The trees
As they reach towards the heavens above
Their leaves of many shades
Whispering in the wind
The secrets of nature's way
The colours that cast the reflections
Of the time
Upon the majestic Earth -
Where the beauty and splendour
Comes together for all eternity.

The magic of the moment
Of a land at peace
Before closing Nature's eyes
Before the winter's sleep -
When the mist and the white ice
In the early morning rise
Covers the valleys of life.

In the new light
Of the morning dawn
Crimson reflections glisten
As the sun breaks
The night shadow into day
The birds singing their soft song
Awakening all life around.

When the time
Comes to close her eyes
Into a peaceful slumber's rest
Before the winter snows
And the crystal flakes
Cover the lands of time -
The living painting of nature.

Susan Russell-Smith

Behold What You See

A starry night,
Birds in flight.
Blooms from seeds planted,
The things we take for granted.
The blind man who holds a rose,
Or sight of which he can only suppose.
Is to make me realise
Of the beauty in the Heaven
And light blue of the sky.
To know of impoverished poor,
Of nations who go to war.
And innocent men and women
Dying by the score.
Then I think of trees in autumn,
And changing of the leaves.
Reminds me of life's situations
And my own trivial tribulations.
So when I have a mood or down
I put on my walking boots
To banish the frown
And admire the beauty to be seen.
For all the things you have ever wanted
Are there around and you take for granted.

Robert Reddy

Who Would I Like To Be?

Sometime ago, I can't think when
Someone on the radio used to ask then
What it was that you liked best
Or who would you be? Be my guest
I think without a shadow of doubt
While I was young and an active Scout
Camping and hiking all over the land
Out in the open made me feel so grand
Best of all was a simple thing
The cold mist in the morning made my legs sting
This I enjoyed and had great fun
But was soon replaced by a very warm sun
If we were lucky and it shone all day
A good active programme would be coming our way
So if ever the question was put to me
Of who do I think I would like to be
Only one answer would I be able to find
It's me, to whom nature has been so kind.

E S Segust

Positive - Uplifting

In your space, when you have the time,
Go find a quiet spot, sit and chime,
Feet on the floor, hands on your lap
How nice it is where you are sat,
Close your eyes in peace as you sleep,
Look at your life, just take a peep,
There's nothing in the world that you can't do,
Yes, all that you want really can come true,
Deeper and deeper, as you are,
You can do anything you want so far,
For you can be that more clever,
Don't let me hear you say never,
As all the world is at your feet,
So everything now you can seek,
Now you will always find peace in your heart,
For a new world in your life you must start,
Always find time for relaxing,
Send all your worries a-faxing,
You can face life as you go,
Look into the face of your foe,
For life is so peaceful and free,
You are everything you can be.

Margaret Burtenshaw-Haines

Thunder

The rain is coming, so I know it's time
To sit in the conservatory and wait for the first drops.
Those dark, menacing clouds will not let us down,
Bursting, seeking a landing site to deposit their cargo.
When it starts to pour, my only thoughts are of you,
And I know you will be thinking of me.
I hold the telephone close to my racing heart,
Waiting for your call to come.
We are on the same wavelength,
Finely tuned, locked into our own secret frequency.
These special moments lift our fragile spirits,
Entwine our souls, blend our youthful hopes.
Too dark for stars to guide us,
But our magnetic bond draws us cosy closer.
I sense your fingers dialling, electric perception,
My joy explodes as I hear the ringing.
Second sight, I know exactly where you are,
What you are wearing, those sighs and smiles.
Only your very secret thoughts evade me,
As we both put on our song in the background.
Conversation is nervous, but the ice is soon broken,
A charm offensive of hurried throwaway lines draw out the laughter.
A special witch's brew chemistry floats us into nirvana,
Promises and pledges made to break at our leisure.
The rain is going so I know it's time,
To move on, get back to the daily grind.
Say our lingering goodbyes and put the telephone down,
Thunder claps our performances, then rumbles on his way.

John Green

A Prayer For Peace

Oh, Father, listen to my prayer
For worldwide peace: a planet where
All manner of humanity
Can live in perfect harmony,
Instead of waging constant wars,
Fighting for some pointless cause.
Let us lay our guns aside,
Drop no more bombs - no genocide.
And, when we feel the hatred rise,
Help us to love, and not despise.
Give us the inner strength we need
To conquer our rapacious greed.
And, once we've gained these attributes
There'll be no reason for disputes.
The overdue peace will prevail -
No more enemies to assail.
Peace on Earth - for this I pray;
And then, please let it stay that way.

Heather D Pickering

Love's Triumph

(for Santosh Rani)

In my moments of recollection
I dream of your soft-footed, tender gait,
So like a shy peahen or a frightened doe,
So very delicate.
The very way you walked
Drove me to desire with pure passion.
Your movement was sheer poetry,
Choreographed with precision.
You performed a ballet
In slow motion.
And when our eyes met,
Alas, for short, solitary moments,
They spoke volumes of love
Which words could never express.
But what are words
When love can be so strong?
Words are weak.
Let silence speak.

The moment that you were conceived
The gentle gods gave you to me.
How else can we explain our love?
It is the hand of destiny.

Amazing are the twists of fate;
But we, my sweet, are fortunate.
We are at last victorious!
Our love has won! Though somewhat late.

Reginald Massey

At A Glance

There he sits
In a corner of the room
Behind glass
A small boy sitting, smiling, always smiling
Emboldened with love invested
But he doesn't move
He cannot
He's fixed in time in an image long ago
And then I blink
He's moved
He's there before me
Yet look how tall and proud he stands
Still emboldened
Love invested shining through
And smiling, always smiling
All of 18 years
Where has it gone?
Where will it go?

The path ahead may be long and winding
Like your artful scribbles long ago
So take time to pause, draw breath
To look, to listen, love and learn
As you interweave the stories
That will become the fabric of your life

And may you be forever smiling,
Smiling as the years unfold . . .

Yvonne Allison

Belief

I do not believe God only
dwells in man-made places,
surrounded by crosses and icons
and saints with wooden faces.

Man tries to capture his belief
and attempts to surround
a chosen piece of land
declaring it to be holy ground.

If you believe what they say,
and accept their ideas,
you will never know God
in a thousand years.

You must not be bound
by superstition and fears,
but lessons you've learned
as you accumulate years.

Things you learn, from
listening to your higher self,
and philosophical ideas,
from books on your shelf.

God had no bounds,
His Spirit is free
to those who seek it
and accept it to be.

Suzanna Wilson

Does It Really Matter?

Raining . . .
feeling as though,
well just as though,
but look on the bright side,
it won't rain forever,
the sun will come out and shine, eventually.

And think, how good, the flowers, grass and trees
are feeling right now.

OK, so you want to go out and play,
you can play tomorrow.
You thought you might take the dog for a walk,
you can take him later.

You want to go shopping,
the shops are not going to close down,
if you don't go today,
look on the bright side,
all you want to do today,
you can do tomorrow.
                              Does it really matter?

Jacqueline Claire Davies

Time To Remember

These were the times he loved the best
As he strolled along the shore
With trousers rolled up
Walking the same stretch as before
Holding tightly on to his hand
His small grandson chatted away
Taking him back to own childhood
When with his own grandpa before them
Had been brought here for the day
The sea to him was magic
On a rough day it came in with a force
But on calm days it was quite lazy
And gently rippled in of course
Now they were back where they had started
Making their way to the train
But promising his small grandson
They assuredly would come again

Daphne Fryer

Sam

You're my day, my night,
You make everything right,
You give me the love that I need,
To get me through my life.

You're my hope, my joy,
Such a wonderful boy,
You make my soul complete,
In a world that is incomplete.

The love that you bring,
Makes my heart want to sing,
I can't believe the gift that you've given,
To bring happiness to a girl like me.

You're my stone, my rock,
The key to my lock,
You listen when needed,
Yet your voice helps to soothe.

To me, you're my life,
I can but hope to be your wife,
To part would not be a question,
My heart could ever consider.

And the most important thing
Of all the above,
Is that I am yours,
And you, my love, are mine.

Lauren Watkins

Friends Forever

Thank you for being my friend
Thank you for all you lend
Not money, you understand
Perhaps a helping hand
Sometimes just an ear
Should I doubt or fear

We've been through thick and thin
We're just like kith and kin
In't good times and in't dire
In't clover and in't mire
Together heart and soul
Two halves that make us whole

Two souls that fit together
These words are but some measure
Of my regard and thankfulness
Without you I'd be in a mess
We're stuck together like glue
God bless, for being you.

Ian Tomlinson

Daffodils

I planted pretty daffodils
along my garden wall
the winter season
was soon to pass
the earth's encrusted
heavy mass
became a brilliant bright
yellow glow
of dancing daffodils
in a row
they swayed and touched
in the cool spring air
a dancing, yellow, brilliant flare
petals tinged with orange trumpets
repeat in every flower
my daffodils so splendidly
contrast from the winter
frosty grasp.

Margery Rayson

Father To Son

It's over in the corner, the door you must take,
I've tried to point it out to you in so many ways,
I've tried each day to show you the way,
You're so inspirational, what can I say?
I love you more and more day by day
It's over in the corner, the door you must take
You laughed high, you laughed low,
Day by day I have seen you grow.
Time is moving by me, and soon you must go.
As the shadows of the evening obscure the day
I've tried to tell you, did you hear me say?
It's over there in the corner, the door you must take.
Good luck, good love, and good will hunting.
You have been my good friend, I will love you forever,
In your life you must always endeavour
To be good, to be true, to always love you,
To rise as the sun, to float like the moon,
To remember me and say, 'See you soon',
To grow old and wise in so many ways,
It's right there in the corner, the door you must take.

Andrew Eddy

Remember A Happy Thought

When you have a happy thought hold it close and tight,
recalling it will lift the dark of any long night,
a thought that touches your heart or makes you smile,
creates a warm feeling when you remember it after a while.

Perhaps it is the hug of a loved one unexpectedly,
the memory of a favourite childhood teddy,
your puppy sleeping on your knee,
or a chat with a friend over a cup of tea.

These little things mean so much,
especially the warmth of a loving touch,
or hearing a kind word or two,
simple things to lift you whenever you feel blue.

Julie Marie Laura Shearing

Facing Depression

Today if you happen to be feeling very low
You need help but know nobody to whom you can go
Life to you is not worth living
It is not possible to see anything to be doing or giving
Sometimes you could get silly thoughts into your head
And start making plans for yourself to be dead
One should remember they will not see death
Until the world-maker decides they draw their last breath

It is well known people will have problems from birth
For if they did not they would not be on this earth
A person should face their problems and be brave
Instead of sitting about wishing they were in their grave

They should remember that life is not all bad
And think of some good events in life that they have had
However it is important not to dwell on the past
About a problem somebody had they feared would always last

The world is full of plenty to see and do
There will be something enjoyable for people all the year through
When a person goes out they never know what they could find
It could be a new hobby or a talk giving them peace of mind
Nobody should sit at home and face their life alone
Housebound people should keep in touch by telephone
Each person should help their neighbour in every way
This will mean everybody has a happy and healthy day

Robert Doherty

New Directions

Despite my human frailty
My loving Lord still welcomed me.
In His wisdom my Father knew
That I must my future think anew
By paths uncertain I would tread
In loving kindness there He led
Then, later, in my silent sorrow
When thinking of the empty morrow
In sadness and with bitter tears
My mind traced back the passing years
I saw my loving Lord had ever been
In my life and yet unseen
Forbidden love, regrets and memories sad
Now my risen Lord bade me be glad
That He my lonely life had filled
With people whose needs o'erspilled
And in serving Him that I would see
The suffering Christ in humanity
Of unforeseen tragedies and deaths unaware
that I would with these people share
And in their points of life so low
I prayed the face of Christ to show
Of their lives, the broken heart
Friend, confidante, I'd become a part
And in those moments hard to cope
The dying Christ became my hope
He was my strength, my certainty
His Resurrection had set me free
And so I thank my Lord above
Who died for me, unbounded love
Whose rising promised yet to me
The promise of eternity
So, to Father, Son and Spirit three
I give thanks and praise your gifts to me.

Brenda Hughes

Farewell, Old Friend

(On the downfall of an ancient apple tree)

One hundred years of fruitfulness,
How sad that it should end like this,
A jagged stump, a twisted branch or two,
Dying leaves, a withered apple peering through.
Faint shadow of the passing years
Of loaded boughs in layered tiers,
Of spreading branches giving shade
To teatime tables often laid
In times when tea was taken after noon.
All those forgotten springs when in full bloom -
Branches spreading,
Bounty shedding,
Countless apples every year.
Then withered leaves, all dead and sere.

And now -
A savage south-west wind, a canker in the heart,
A gentle tearing and then they part,
Two huge branches, south and east,
Bowed down and landed with a crashing sigh,
A wall of foliage ten feet high
Vainly reaching to the sky.

So farewell, old friend,
All things must end,
But maybe I'll strike a twig or two
And happily, you may renew.

Eileen M Lodge

Untitled

Now the day is sending the darkness is falling fast
Dear Lord please help me to fulfil my task
Thank You for helping me along life's way
To see yet another perfect day
The sunlight and the shadows are closing in on me
Please help and guide me for all eternity
I am so grateful that I'm still here
Every day is precious to me and I know You're near
Put your faith in God, He will never fail you
He will be there every day to see you through
There are many roads to take in life before we find our way
The Lord will always be with you every single day

Enid Skelton

A Magi Remembers

My friends are dead, I have grown old remembering
The strange journey we took together following a star,
As we crouched together in the night,
Talking and warming ourselves in firelight,
Trying to understand, to fathom the meaning.
In early dawn light, into the saddle springing,
Travelling always onward, seeking again
Each night following the star.
It stopped, we came to a humble place,
A child on his mother's breast.
A child, such a child, God's glory manifest.
I remember now, ecstasy filled our souls,
Here was the answer to all men's fears and woes.
What became of the child? He grew God's love to teach,
Healed the sick, went far, the broken heart to reach.
The so-called keeper of God's holy law.
Blind leading blind, never the joyous message saw
Said he blasphemed against God, cried, 'Crucify',
Hating him for destroying an outward creed.
The darkness of death, on him had no holding,
Death's chains he broke, gave us light everlasting.
The light, we the magi, were seeking always.
We saw God's wondrous, glorious ways.
It was long ago, I in joy remembering,
In peace, content to die in God's glory,
Knowing the light beyond the grave.

B Kerby

The Lift

I like to be uplifted,
To be higher than a tree,
To look out and to ponder
On how can all this be?

I like to be uplifted,
And everything I can see
Makes me think and wonder
How and why can all this be?

One day we'll know the answer
So there's no point in worrying about that,
I will get on with the day-to-day living
And looking out from my top floor flat.

Rachel E Joyce

Untitled

Look inside yourself
    Deep within your heart
      Find love
        Where it is
          Forgive . . .
    And make a fresh start.

All the dreams; reality
    That once tore your world apart.

Togetherness; strength; love and
      Understanding . . . *peace.*

A brand new start.

Suzanne Kemp

Depression

When you're feeling depressed and blue
Don't fade away into a dream
Which you know to be untrue
Do not let yourself surmise
And think things are worse than they are
So that mountains arise from molehills
And things look black as tar
It's better to face your problems
Take them one by one
And try to sort out a solution
Until those worries are gone
Everyone gets depressed at times
Remember you're not on your own
Share your thoughts with someone else
And you won't feel so alone.

Violetta Jean Ferguson

Happiness

Oh such joy and happiness,
surrounds me every day.
For I have three special friends,
that take me out to play.
You may think I'm disadvantaged,
with two legs and I haven't got a tail.
But fun I have and laughs galore,
Through meadows and woodland trail.
Never mind if it's muddy, that's
the time Springers love the best.
Diving in the river, there
is no time for rest.
We meet the nicest people,
and all of us agree.
Four-legged friends keep us fit
and happiness comes free.
Such unconditional devotion
for they only want to please.
Guard and watch over me and
worry if I hide behind the trees.
The only thing they ask for is
some food and a comfy bed.
A good groom and a cuddle
while they rest their poor tired head.
When the day is over and
we snuggle by the fire.
So happy and contented
we have our heart's desire.
Who would want to change things?
Certainly not I.
I love my dogs, I love my life,
So much with joy I cry.

Irene Keeling

Arrival

I cannot see the sea
But I hear it
The ebbing
The flowing
The gentle crashing of waves upon the shore dispersing the multitude
of tiny hard grains
Displacing their pattern

I cannot see the wind
But I feel it
The warmth
The coolness
The unceasing movement changing and swirling the earth, blowing
and bowing all
Moulding their shape

I cannot see the love
But I know it
The caring
The sharing
The invisible bond of generosity weaving through the hearts of
strangers who become friends
Replenishing their lives

I cannot see the peace
But I breathe it
The calmness
The holiness
The spiritual essence travelling within and around each beautiful being
Surrounding their soul

Val Duggan

Spring

Hush! Silence electrified,
Trees glisten with opaque pearls,
Shimmering in the sun,
Leaves, freshly opened by the rain
Greedily drink this soft warm nectar,
Stillness all around,
Awakening after the long hibernation
Birds hardly dare utter the song
They will sing as
Some long ago memory stirs.
I breathe gently,
An intruder
Afraid to disturb this magic,
Aware of the beauty,
The stillness around me,
I see apple-green buds unfurling
A pink-tipped cherry
Shyly showing its petticoat
Like a bride,
She will soon burst in glory
Unveiling herself to her groom,
Springtime is again upon us!

Val Aspin

Sometimes I Play Mozart

Sometimes I play Mozart
just to be with you,
young again,
when youth's campus-green spread before us
with horizons clear as topaz blues and
white marshmallow clouds
neither checked the sun nor
canopied one star-sapphire-studded night.

Sometimes I play Mozart
just to be with you,
young again,
when youth's blushed dew-rose dawn and
evening flushed warm ruby hues and
anywhere we wandered glinted opal-gold,
silver-new, a magic-fluted romance down
grand garden paths where you and I were led.

Sometimes I play Mozart,
young again,
when our youths' magic music fused with his
and light-scented spring seemed no softer
nor so near than close for us to be.
Yes, sometimes I play Mozart to relive
when all your smiling happy joy was
just to be with me.

Edgar Wyatt Stephens

Father's Day

I hear the prattle and
settle in my seat,
the chirrups from the
kitchen tells it all.
Quiet has gone
and joy is being spun
like gossamer wings.
They're a perfect pair
made to match,
from the first
they seemed to
be in happy flight
fluttering, enfolding
floating at my side
as butterflies
raising me up to
be the hero
to be the superman
they give me wings.

Sheila O'Hara

Dear Friend

Soon you shall embark adventures new -
Unknown paths your feet shall tread.
But locked within that brave-faced shell I know
You hide secret anticipation fiercely embraced by fear.
But Friend, you're driven by determination draped
In patience, and I just know you will greet Success.

When sleep does not come for you as you lie in worry-wonderment
Of unfamiliar people and what days may or may not bring;
Just remember that nameless faces are future friends and
How many lives, long for the element of surprise you're about

to gain.

I understand that your journey won't be an ocean of smooth sailing . . .
And when you stand 'beat' as you face a mountain when you

expected a hill
I'll be one step ahead, my hand outstretched to help you to the top.
Or if you have a race against time I will carry you should you

fall behind.
Even if you're simply feeling lost, with a road in front harbouring

eerie shadows.
I'll be there, whether it is in mind, memory or by your side.

Jessica E Stapleton

Totality

(Totality is about the Solar Eclipse of 1999 seen in its longest spell of total eclipse in Ozora, Hungary. We shared the experience with people all over Europe, including friends who were far apart but much loved, all watching the same event.)

Bright gold eaten
Discs collide
Slide across and slowly darken
Immense space between;
Only shadows
Cast by worlds are seen.

Noonday sunset
Evening sky
Petals close, birds drop
Stars prick blue;
Cloud and colour luminous
Black circle ringed in fire
Frozen time.

No time and no place
Empty space,
Orbiting in paradox
From grass to sky.
And I know
Somewhere
You see this too.
The nothing moments spin slowly by
As I turn with you.

Immense space between
Only shadows cast
From you to me remain.
A chill-drop of totality
This midday fear, this loss
This endless wandering
Of worlds.

Two minute passing
Diamond flare
We
Have seen this together
Outside of endings and of time
And can go on living
Knowing this

Knowing this
That time removed,
We shared beauty.
And there is nothing more
That I can give to you;
Hoping somewhere
As that moment passed
You felt it too.

Alyson Stoneman

It's Better To Have Loved And Lost

It's better to have loved and lost
Than not having loved at all
Coz I must learn my mistakes from the past
To answer the call of my soul
And avoid making similar mistakes in the future
Coz where there's love there's pain
And that's the grand design of Mother Nature;
I answer the call of love again and again
Coz no matter how many times I am burnt
I can't escape the clutches of my desire.
Lessons are designed to be learnt
But when logic is consumed by fire
And reason falls head over heels
Caught in the headlights of a brand new love;
I sacrifice and compromise all my ideals
But only Master Time rises to prove
What is false and what is real.
I discard my mind and swim with my heart
Oblivious of what lies beyond the shore
Will I find love or have my heart ripped apart?
And if I should fall at least I gave it my all.

Joseph M Nthini

Beautiful Day

This morning I felt like singing quietly
'Morning has broken
like the first morning'.
It must have been like that
dew on the grass
sunbathing creation.
This lovely morning
when all is so still.

'Mine is the sunlight,
mine is the morning'.
Yes it's all mine
mine to partake
mine to enjoy.

Shirley Ludlow

Kristen The Rising Star

*(A tribute to the 13-year-old daughter of dear friends in USA for her magnificent
performance in a Christmas play in 2002)*

'Twas Christmas in two thousand two, I saw
Miss Kristen Perry acting in a play:
'The Bestest Christmas Pageant Ever', for
The Fountains at Boca Ciega Bay.
The play revolved around Nativity,
It gave us all much thought about His birth:
Itself a lesson in humility,
For humble we may be, yet still have worth.
Miss Kristen, as Beth Bradley, played the lead,
With clarity of diction told the tale
So perfectly, no prompter had to read.
Performing so, the meaning could not fail
To register. Miss Kristen, you'll go far:
You've proved for sure that you're a rising star!

Christopher Head

Life In God

And the bread and wine of life stand still
A token of what will be
Where we live in one and all
And we see the service pass
And the memory of the dear departed
As we see her memory committed to God
To look after our dear departed sister
And we speak of the end of death

And the choir begin to sing
About the bread of life
And the voices rise and rise
As the tambourine sounds
'And I will raise you up on the last day'
As the glittering crescendo roar
As the triumph sounds across the hall
And the hall beats with the sound of the voices
In a moment of transcendent time
Where all is suspended
Before the triumph of the Almighty

And in this glory stands the truth
Death is not the end but a triumph into another world
Where pain and despair will be gone
Where we know the promise
That life will be different
And we will all be raised up on the last day

Alasdair Sclater

Friendships

Friendships precious and valuable
So delicate,
Never sellable
Always our mate.

From God, friends are a true gift
Never, will a friendship break
A true friend always ready to lift -
You out of a mess you make.

Ramandeep Kaur

Prayer To The Word Made Flesh

Jesus, we always want to exclude,
to reject those who are different,
to marginalise whole groups,
to cold-shoulder those who don't walk with us,
to keep safe distances and erect
sanitised barriers to love and desire
lest they should humanise us.

But You, Jesus, You say,
'Do not forbid him who uses my name.'
'You don't know what spirit you are of.'
You cast down walls of partition,
You embrace the despised, the neglected,
You risk being called drunkard, glutton,
You share the parties of the poor,
You dine at the outcast's table,
You welcome the sinner to Your kingdom.

Make us, Lord, like You,
accepting, embracing, including,
until, with You, we may say,
'There is nowhere I should not go,
no one I should not love.'

Derek Rawcliffe

A Wave Of Love

A wave of love approached my boat,
A fresh breeze surrounded me nicely,
My memories should be allowed to float
And to sail away with the wave slowly.

My boat can't find the right direction,
It moves freely back and forth - I keep balance.
Any returns are out of the question,
I take delight in the smoothing silence . . .

But the wind is stronger and stronger,
I have to master the rudder to survive,
But the frothy wave is higher and higher,
I was washed ashore, yet I'm still alive . . .

Jolanta Gradowicz

The Gift

Life has its problems - fate deals its blows
What we have coming nobody knows.
Each day's a gift unwrapped as we wake,
Some days delight us - some bring heartache.
When times are hard, we learn how to cope,
Working and struggling - clinging to hope,
Building our backbones - showing our grit,
Strength through misfortune will conquer it.

Each day's a gift - unwrap it with pride,
There's always something worthwhile inside -
Friendship and laughter, music and song,
Good books to read when dark nights are long,
Sunshine in winter - flowers in spring,
So many pleasures nature can bring.
Moments of sorrow - happiness too -
Each day's a gift presented to you.

Joy Saunders

A New Life!

We are selling our house,
What a big deal!
After 10 years,
How do I feel?

We are moving abroad
To the Emerald Isle,
Going to build a new house,
And stay for a while.

We are splitting the family,
How do I feel?
They are very supportive,
But what, when it's real?

The older three are settled,
In homes of their own,
The two younger ones are coming,
To our new home.

There'll be new friends to make,
And new jobs too,
The land is up a mountain
And oh! What a view!

So when we've built
And settled in,
And we've realised our dream,
The kids can frequently visit us,
And we'll be together, now and again.

So really then there's nothing lost,
They are grown-ups after all,
With PCs and the Internet,
We really won't be apart at all.

So now I've given it some serious thought,
I'm no longer so afraid,
Just looking forward to our new build,
And the foundations are finally laid.

Jennifer Collins

My Heart And I

In my heart I keep all my secrets safe
Everything there is calm with no haste
Memories in there are stored to keep
When in bed I think of them as I sleep
The secrets my heart holds are just for me
That I alone can enter and see
I keep my memories no one will share
My personal thoughts are locked in there
The love of my life is there tucked away
Who will know for I will never say?
My secret heart is as strong as a fort
Full up with my sweetest thoughts
No one can probe or look in and see
For it is only I that holds the key.

L A G Butler

Did You . . .?

Did you make someone laugh today or maybe just a smile,
or offer to do shopping and carry it a mile?
Did you help someone cross the road - someone you never knew
or hold a door open - for someone to follow you?

Did you send Mother's birthday card exactly on the date
or search through piles of others, for one that says 'I'm late'?
When did you *take* a bunch of flowers - a visit means a lot
or did you find a lame excuse, because you just forgot?

Did you do something willingly - without a second thought
or did you need persuading then - 'do because you ought'?
Did you 'have second thoughts' and hold back a biting word
or did you say just what you thought - then pray they never heard?

Did you scold son or daughter for something they had done
when really *you* weren't happy - *they* were having fun?
Then did you say 'I'm sorry' when tears came to their eyes
or did you look the other way and not apologise?

If you did one good thing today - you get a golden star,
if in a month you did a lot, you get a star - with 'bar'.
If you did not even think of one, then start - it's not too late
because you need a *million* to pass the golden gate.

Jim Pritchard

Nature

As the trees reach for the sky above
The Father surrounds us with His love
The birds sing out their joyful song
As the sun comes out to warm the Earth

The butterfly flies swiftly by
Her wings feel the sun's warmth
She seeks a flower where she can rest
And safely hide from all harm

At times we need to look around
To see the beauty that surrounds us
Lawns and flowers tended with care
Sun and rain sent from above

So as we lift our faces to Heaven
We give thanks for each new day
And pray that you will guide us
Along life's great highway

Brenda Charles

A Lakeside Experience

Sunshine, glistening on the rippling surface of the lake,
Surrounding the stately cruiser waiting patiently to take
A horde of trusting passengers on a memorable tour,
Around the bays and interesting places by the shore.

Nearly one hour passes for enjoying all the view,
Whilst the people on the top deck idly steam and stew!
A gentle breeze just breaking up bright particles of sun
As nature at its loveliest is pleasing everyone.

Back on terra firma where rows of tables stand,
It's hard to eat a sandwich with swans and ducks around;
Pecking here and shoving there they scrabble for first place
Till one large bird exerts himself and fills up all the space.

Driving down a lakeside lane, hugging the coastal line,
Cool water stretches along one side; on the other, fir forests and pine.
Away from the busy city street, alone with sweet, twittering birds,
Each beauty spot reached, with each little beach, sights too
glorious for words.

Water springs from high above, descending several miles.
In many a wood and country path and over rustic stiles
The eager walker climbs, to see a gushing waterfall
Glinting its way from rocks to stones and grasses straight and tall.

One brief moment of time in God's plan, for multitudes of lives,
The thrill of a truly wondrous world, with its greatness
and grandeur, arrives
To fill the soul with stress-free thoughts and clear the cluttered mind.
Spellbound, as majestic mountains breathe peace to all mankind.

A Audrey Agnew

Fledgling Day

Stand still
and hold the moment in your hand,
as time
skelters through fragile fingers,
to store
life's story in patterned pictures.
Leaving
shades of yesterday to fade away,
reach out
and feel the strength of being,
warmed by
rainbow colours rich in promise.
Waking
the fledgling day hovers expectantly,
waiting
for you to fly.

Shirley Johnson

Thoughts At The Close Of The Day

The evening shadows are falling, my day's work is over,
The day had been a day full of action,
I try to reconcile my actions with long-held beliefs,
Hoping that my thoughts will provide some satisfaction.

As I am thinking my mind is filled with doubt,
I cannot be sure if my objective has been achieved,
I know that in many ways, I have been successful,
But, in other ways I know I have been deceived.

I tell myself that many things are impossible,
But, my thoughts tell me that with a little effort on my part,
I could have done a lot more to impress my neighbours,
And could have fulfilled the longings in my heart.

To achieve objectives in part can never be enough,
To achieve our full potential must surely be our aim,
We must strive to achieve real satisfaction,
And to become a winner in life's game.

Sleep does not come easy to a trouble mind,
Sleep does not come easy to a mind filled with regret,
We have to work hard to fulfil our potential,
Sleep will only come when we can forget.

We must try to forget the failures in our life,
Concentrate our thoughts on the things we have achieved,
Resolve to do much better in the future,
To take advantage of the truths we have perceived.

Our concerns will lessen as we think about our success,
When we allow positive thoughts to fill our head,
In this way peace will sublimate our thinking,
At the end of the day when we retire to our bed.

Ron Martin

Easy Pickings

Very near the surface in the warm sunshine,
Little tadpoles swimming in the garden pool
Are spied by Mrs Blackbird as she takes a drink
And, pecking some, the tasty meal really makes her think!

'Good,' says Mrs Blackbird, or so she seems to say,
'I'll hop around the garden and then come back again.
These are easy-pickings, as good as juicy worms,
I can have some lovely meals, on such pleasant terms.'

This, she did, yes, several times
Until, at last, she found
That the rock where she'd been standing
Was, somehow, not around!

Bewildered now, she looked down
On water, too deep for her, she knew
And yet, determinedly she tried to reach
Those tadpoles, still in view.

When, at last, all efforts failed,
She lifted high her head,
Flicked her tail and with disdain
Drank from the water-bowl instead!

Agnes Hickling

Playing Shop

I went to buy a lolly
From the kindergarten store.
But it was just a ping-pong ball
Stuck on to a straw.

I asked them for a comic
Like 'Spot' or 'Fireman Sam',
But all they had was 'Woman's Realm'
And 'Cosmo-poli-tan'.

I thought I'd buy some sausages
To take home for my tea.
But they were made of plasticine
And looked quite green to me.

I went home empty-handed,
Bought nothing in the end.
It's just as well; two Smartie tops
Was all I had to spend!

Carol Byram

George Of England

Our banter-loving landlord sounds better in the open air!
His bosom buddy Mick, will always run out with Kenny's deckchair.
Then there's Ace lugubrious king of the quiz, and his brash style.
What is changing that well worn craggy face, could it be a smile?

Janette dotes on her son and daughter Georgia, they are a fine team
And that gentle giant Phil, I love to watch him beam.
Terry the red-headed Viking, with a pint he's entranced.
John and the love story, how many has Julie romanced?

This brings us to Alan, on the floor he's quite a prancer.
Pretty Lisa loves her role, a different kind of dancer.
So to the motorbike gang, they remind me of velociraptors,
Strangers to the word beauty, I'll christen them the Jurassic Chapters.

Plod is loyal and dry-witted, but was red-carded by the ref,
That infamous day, when he admonished and astonished Little Steph!
This girl echoes your thoughts, brings the place alive.
Confuse Stephanie quickly, before her magical mouth hits overdrive.

Sue our landlady loves dominoes, and is an excellent cook.
To describe the great characters here, I'd need a book.
Life can be boring, so a touch of mischief can be appealing.
It may be a joy to pull someone's leg, but never hurt a feeling!

Michael Malam

Rays Of Light

Little rays of light
that's what you are
bringing sunshine into our lives,
you're a pair of roses
that are so beautiful.

You play with each other
as you sit upon the floor
looking so sweet and innocent,
you're my little rays of light
lighting up my life.

You look up at me
for guidance and love,
I hold your tiny hands,
my hands fit yours like a glove.

I've watched you both
since you were born
but you're growing up so fast,
it amazes me that I have
two beautiful young daughters
who are my pride and joy.

Chris T Tanithe

Brethren

(I dedicate this poem to all my friends; I call you, 'Brethren')

I have a story to write
and an example to cite
because of you people
you are truly noble
I can now agree that friends are born
and not made
I pray our link will never fade
till the end of the age
It is difficult to find one like you anywhere
and I wonder if there is any somewhere.

Thanks for your support and comfort
instead of rejection, you gave me attention
you can never be forgotten
for in my heart, your names are written
when things were difficult to cope
you gave me hope
Oh what joy I find with you
you people are like a sweet haven
great is your reward in Heaven.

Poku Michael Kwadwo

Faith

Faith is believing
Without knowing why
A precious gift from God
That money cannot buy

Faith is believing
That God is by our side
Leading us on the right path
When we choose Him for our guide

Faith is believing
When everything goes wrong
There will be a reason
In our weakness God is strong

Faith is believing
That only God knows best
Offering our lives to Him
His power in us will rest

Jackie Graham

A Forever Friend

When times of sorrow come,
and come they will.
Don't give up hope
let your heart be still.

You're never ever alone
as you pass through this life.
There is a friend who,
for you gave *His* life.

He'll never leave you
He's always there,
keeping you safe
with His love and care.

Don't ever give up
just give God a prayer.
He's always your friend
so please don't despair.

Julie Brown

Incredible Journey

There's a glade of shaded rest, just up ahead
As I journey this path with awe, often dread
In the distance rays of sun, beaming through
Maybe tomorrow, I may visit this place too

Onward now with plenty to do, much to see
Not much time at all, to take this all in for me
Over the hill the weather's always stormy rain
I know I've to go there, sometime, once again

Yet should I veer left, the road's cold frosty ice?
This is somewhere to steer clear, not very nice
To the right, joy and laughter, rings in blue sky
Lifting one's heart and spirit, taking a soul high

This all started off, with a beaming ray of light
Smiles of pleasured laughter, and endless delight
Yet everywhere I go, nowhere seems the same
And some places I often visit, time and time again

Journey end still a choice, two paths to choose
They say choose this right, as one's much to lose
Ups and downs, joy, heartache, bitterness, strife
Sunshine, rain, cold snaps the weathers of life

C R Slater

To My Sons

Throw yourselves upon the world,
Whatever you endeavour.
Keep face and keep your faith,
Dismiss all thoughts of failure.
Beware of envy, pride and bigotry,
These rogues will not inspire you,
They are gifts of Satan.
Cultivate your goodness,
Don't look for easy options.
By always showing kindness
You'll receive more than you give.
Let no one call it weakness,
Always help the underdog.
Keep a ready smile to greet each day
Don't be ashamed to laugh or cry . . .
For when God hears those things
It's just as if you pray.
If you remember this,
Then without exception,
All men will call you friend.

Laszlo Clements

An Ode To The Young At Heart

Look at me and you will see that I am old
each line etched on my face, is a story told.
My body is slow to function, my strength just saps away
it sometime seems difficult, just to make it through each day.

This picture is just a falsehood, this is not the real me
in my eyes you'll find, a wild spirit waiting to be free.
For in my mind I am young, a lad of twenty-three
life has just started and is unexplored territory.

In my imagination I roll back the years
where I find love and laughter and just a few tears.
Each new day I treasure, there is never time enough
to do those things that need doing, that fill life's overflowing cup.

So here's to long liveability and to the road as yet untrod
we will march along to our own time, to the end, until we meet our
God.
We must keep on marching until we reach our goal
live our years with no fears and keep our spirits whole.

William T Ahern

A Special Place

I watched the sun kiss stone lions
dripping from the granite chancel.
It crept along regimental pews,
and devoured the darkness before it.
Footsteps echoed the quietness,
scraping cement flagstones
where generations of history
lay in the depths of its bosom.
Embedded in bare walls,
tombs of dust slept the centuries.
Here they must remain
in their underworld of sacred silence.
I could sense them. I could feel them.
I shivered slightly, and focused on
fresh flower displays,
a living corner of light and Holy care.
Their perfume spraying summer
into the chilled air.
The longer I stood inhaling
this magnificent building,
the more I realised how small I had become.
Yet to be here, standing among
the sacred and the ancient
sent a power so extreme
that all breath and life vanished.
Baptised into the essence of this place.
This House of God, this very special place.

Josephine Duthie

Grey Morning

I wake up
Another day's dawn
It's cold
It's wet
It's miserably uninviting.
I rise
I bathe
I dress
It's not what I want to be doing.
I eat
I drink
I leave
What is this life all about?
I arrive
I sit down
I switch on
Office workers everywhere.
I press buttons
I write letters
I print papers
It's time for coffee -
Whoopee!
Who's finished the crossword?
Who's watched EastEnders?
Who's bought a new dress?
Who's going on holiday?
Where are the photos?
Show me your wedding plans
Show me your new house
What colour paint?
This is what life's about.
Isn't it great?

Sue Reilly

Our Love

Eternal as the hills
fresh as the morning mists
and like the morning mists
      it mutates
      evaporates
is crushed
in the daily rush
of busy-ness

until
in the evening stillness
it drops rippling rings
into the deep pools
of our hearts

Harold Wonham

Keep On Going

When you feel downbeat and think all is lost
Please take heart my friend cos Jesus paid the cost
Died for all mankind so you can have eternal life
Look ahead there's an end to all this strife
Philippians 4.13 says one can do all things
Rising above circumstances like an eagle with its wings
Of course the problem still exists, it's not pie in the sky
Taking eyes off the bad time gives a natural high
A view from the mountain tops puts things in their place
Restoring contempt and a smile upon the face
Put things in their context even when life gets colder
Focusing on the Lord and you will get bolder
God's children are loved, He's mindful of your disappointment
He'll soon show up because disappointment becomes
                                        His appointment
Attentive to your cry whatever the time of day
When you get down to pray help is on its way
Things change if you can see it it's just for a season
Just for that keep on going that's not a bad reason

Shaun O'Grady

Sunrise

I was looking through my window
as the dawn began to break
the dark of night was fading
a new day would soon awake
as clouds began to lighten
faint colours caught my eye
and for a while my thoughts were drawn
to the magic in the sky

I saw the morning sunrise
it was my greatest thrill
as she rose up in full glory
from behind a distant hill
soft colours as a rainbow
swept across the sky
no artist here could ever paint
like the one who reigns on high

Sylvia Quayle

Surfing Without A Net

A buoyant wave,
bounces jerkily,
speedily approaching.
He waits patiently,
biding his time,
coiled like a spring.
Then sharply leaps,
swerving downwards,
lodging safely below,
the swirling water.

The breaking swell,
engulfs him inside
an eerie darkness.
Flecks of yellow,
flickering fitfully,
in the distance.
Swiftly he surges forward,
gamely staying upright,
pondering his fate.

A gamut of emotions,
filter through his mind.
Fear, anxiety, excitement.
Then finally ecstasy,
as he safely soars,
into brilliant sunlight.
This is his moment.
The moment when he
conquers the danger.
The moment which makes
it all, worthwhile.

Paul Kelly

Lilies

They stand
in the clear-glass vase;
taller than the other flowers . . .
two lilies,
his favourites,
by his photograph.

Pure white petals opened wide
to reveal pale green stamens . . .
orange dust-covered pods
balanced on their tips.

They smell of wood smoke,
Have you ever noticed?
Memories of long-ago days.

They stand among freesia,
dark green aspidistra leaves;
carnations and daisies . . .

pink, yellow, orange, blue.

Spring colours
heralding new life -
new beginnings -
and the drawing to an end
of a long, hard winter.

Pat Spear

Slug

Oh slug
      thou foul being
              creeping
            slithering
across the patio
            towards
                my beautiful plants.
                      But you are a creature of God
                      just like me
                      and if some people
                      see me as a
                      foul slug
                      well, I know that I am not.
                          So I will not
                exterminate you.
I will let you slither
            and ooze
              and hope
                  that the plants survive . . .

Valerie Sutton

Each New Day

Time forever each day must go
Like a gentle river in constant flow
Each day is new to everyone
Cheer every second with smile and song.
Greet the moment of each new dawn
Like the rose that blooms; it gives perfume
Give a smile to all the people you meet
Wish them well, as the moment fleets.
In passing of day memories are made
Some will be joyful, and others sad
To keep in our heart, good and bad
Thank the Lord in Heaven above
For living experience of having love.
Love is a blessing that helps us through
It strips the anger from our thoughts
And guides us through so many storms.
See only the good in what people do
Cast out the hate that follows you
Angels of light will guide you through.

Joan Prentice

The Best Of Everything

The best teacher, is the teacher who challenges you,
Doesn't shield you from the harsh realities of life,
But instead gives you tools with which to cope.

The best student, is the student that listens,
Who learns what the teacher has to teach
And grows within that wisdom.

The best friend, is the friend who is there for you,
Comforts you when you need it, shares your good times
And is always there when you call.

The best way to live your life,
Is not to run from the challenges,
But accomplish what the teacher has decreed will define you.

The best repayment you can give,
Is to learn your lessons well
And put them into practical action.

The best God, is the one who doesn't smother,
Or demand more than you can do
And only asks that you try your best.

The best moment, is when you realise,
You've been given the privilege,
To know that all these things have been offered freely.

The best reward, is knowing that you've been allowed to try
And no matter how many times you fail,
He responds with the best gift. His love.

Anne Marie Latham

A Woman Of Strength

When I glance back to the past,
When I focus on glimpses of what happened,
When I see snapshots
I see children close knit,
I see a mother bravely trying to keep afloat,
I enjoy watching her iron so firmly
Trying to instil values into us kids
Barely comprehending.
I too was impressed by her care.
I loved her meekness.
She was there for us.
There was no one else in the kitchen
But she was between us and the vagaries of life.
We relied on her and she taught me.
That woman had deep strength.
She mattered to me a great deal.
Her mind was worthy of consideration;
Worthy to listen to and reflect and
In later years for me to acquire wisdom.
In that simple kitchen
Was a great deal of richness.
It was a loving spirit despite all her faults.
She tried to smooth away our cares.
She made an indelible impression especially
On later choices in life.

Barry Broadmeadow

Untitled

My Lord has taught me to tell a true prayer
While I was waiting for Him endlessly,
In town, park, or rosy coloured glade,
He has given me gifts beyond imagining -
My Lord has taught me to tell a true prayer.

He has sat beside me on cold winter's nights,
And soothed my brow with His hand,
And spoke with a soft voice into my ear.

He said to leave words behind, and move,
While I was waiting for Him endlessly,
My Lord has taught me to tell a true prayer.

I will keep His words silently, and bow,
And offer nothing new. To far countries
I will go to sing: my Lord's words are true.

Alen Ontl

Galactic Theme Park

A soul full of rhythm,
A heart full of sound,
A mind full of meaning,
The words dance around.
Keep time with the music
In two, three, four,
From Big Bang to Big Crunch
Learn to read the score
Of life's unfolding symphony,
Suns, atoms too,
The whole amazing process
Which led up to you!
And even if Our Maker
Likes His face to hide,
Don't let His coldness grieve you,
Just enjoy the ride
On galactic roller coaster
Spinning round in space;
When the mind's doors are wide open,
You can feel the pace.
Just greet the sun with aubades
When his light grows strong,
Bid farewell in gnat-dance-twilight,
Sing your evensong.
Birth, growth, death, sweet oblivion,
so the cycle goes'
And is death the door to higher life?
God only knows!
But inside our space-time-capsule
Searching eyes may find
Vital clues to all the answers
Which lie in His mind.
Use the power within you
To unlock the door,
As the pages in The Book of Life
Turn evermore!

Alan Swift

A Broken Wing

I stumbled once upon a sight
A heavenly body bereft of flight.
An angel with a broken wing
A limp and damaged hanging thing.
Teardrops falling, his only sound
In the knowledge he was Earthly bound.
With pride and grace the pain he bore
Heaven's sweet guardians I do adore.
To comfort him I tried my best
Once bandaged, I told him to rest.
Through the night I sat in place
To watch the pain ease from his face.
In early dawn my head did nod
The angel pure then met with God.
A touch of hand, his wing made good,
It worked as well as ever it should.
When my eyes did flutter awake
An empty bed, my heart did break.
Bandages rolled were all I found
A single feather upon the ground.
When comes the time for me to die
I'll clutch that feather and say goodbye.
I know to Heaven I will ascend
Within the arms of my angel friend.

Ceri D D Griffiths

The Olive Tree

In quiet contemplation I sit beneath a canopy of silver leaves,
searching for a moment of tranquillity and peace.

Above me a myriad of precious jewels are ripening in the sun,
inviting me to stay and fix my silent gaze upon.

I close my eyes and speak to my Creator through my prayers,
His holy presence capturing all worries, doubts and cares.

Resting by this tree that bears the scars of nature's sufferings,
I sense its boughs enfolding me in love and humble offerings.

These verdant fruits are but a symbol of the gifts we may receive,
when we cry, 'Abba Father,' as the spirit intercedes.

Elizabeth Mason

My Guardian Angel

I felt the breath of an angel,
As a wisp of gossamer lace,
And a sound, like the swish of angelic wings
Stirred the air above my face.
No shape saw I, nor heard a voice
Yet its presence was all around,
My guardian angel, close at hand
Hovered near the ground.

When the mist of sleep envelops me
Thoughts transpose to dreams,
Heavy eyelids droop on cheeks
The moon sends forth her beams.
Then do I sense the angel of God
As I pray before I sleep
Knowing, dear Lord, all will be safe
As the vigil of night it keeps.

I give thee thanks for life, for love
For sight, to hear, to smell
For husband, families held dear
For all on Earth who dwell.
Give peace to war-torn nations
Lord of all, I pray
That our guardian angels watch over us
To protect us night and day.

And when the day dawns
For the angel of death
To take my soul on high
Let me go, unafraid
To a place that's been saved
By the angel - for me - in the sky.

Pamela Carder

Churchbagging

Churches are an item you can count on,
there's one at least in every place you go:
the smallest village has its church or chapel,
sometimes there's an organ - that can go;
occasionally, nearly all its notes are present,
at times, no stops drop off, when they're pulled out,
but stay intact, untouched by rot. It's pleasant
to be here when there's no one else about.
You might just meet the rector, priest or vicar,
always keen to indulge his shell-like ear,
get you or yours to play - a little quicker
than he's used to at the hands of some old dear
who's more a pianist really. Here you'll find
a sanctum that can bring you peace of mind.

A church shuts out the hubbub of the world,
helps you focus and contain your contemplation,
lets you concentrate on problems that have hurled
themselves in your direction. Meditation
can be balm to calm the savage hurt within you:
here you can voice your cares and fears freely,
use the peace and quiet that your nature's kin to,
without the usual self-reproach. Ideally,
the like should be a commonplace each day,
in church or not: in practice, it's not so;
so if this respite helps you on your way,
then seize the opportunity and go,
with clear conscience and an open mind,
away awhile. Leave cluttered cares behind.

Adrian Brett

Still Time To Listen

You say life has passed you by
Bemoan your lot, give up and die
Or take refuge from the world by hiding
Close down the mind to gloom abiding
To take this path is an easy fall
Taken by many who lost God's call
His call too soft as they chased the dollar
Caught up in avarice he needed to holler
Selfishness is a cancerous cell
It will eat from within, leaving a shell
This downward slide is a voyage untrue
And your only clue is your fellow travellers and crew
Look back to the love and warmth from your past
What happened and why is the die really cast?
Of course not, there's hope if you again strain to hear
Open your heart; hear His call through the tear
Feel the glow touch the warmth as you draw close to your peers
Is that a smile and the first one for years?
Man's spirit is Olympian he made it to succeed
Hear! the call is louder now, just follow his creed.

Charles Keeble

Be Strong

Be strengthened by the words of God,
They are the food of the spirit.
Let each word fill you with joy,
The joy of the Lord is without limit.

When disappointments drag you down,
To the depths of deep despair,
Take comfort in the knowledge
That you are in God's care.

Comfort will replace the sorrow,
Of lost opportunities,
God will give you another chance,
He controls your destiny.

When you need to see a friendly face,
On a dark and dismal day,
Keep focused on God's promises,
He will direct your way.
Be strong in the Lord, trust His words.

Joyce Warden

Life Goes On

Life can be a dream that seldom lasts
And for some, it's pretty dour at times.
When a loved one leaves before their span.
The rhythm of life slowly starts to grind.

Tense expressions and gritted teeth,
Are all we can use to keep a grip.
The fragile mind just hanging on.
Praying: hoping that it won't flip.

But angels, or whatever they are
Appear on the scene in myriad ways.
To cast their magic across the mind
And begin to ease the agonising days.

The darkened soul begins to clear.
Gestures from all around appear.
The first cracked smile will gently break.
The pain and sorrow slowly disappear.

It may be one special friend or even two,
Who cracks the lock and opens up the door.
Beyond this Earth the absent one will smile
And slowly, happiness returns once more.

A special kind of joy will fill the void.
Not better, just different than before.
Not perfect love, but a comfort still,
Will heal two souls: or maybe more.

John Troughton

Changes

Change is inevitable.
With time comes experience and the knowledge to survive.
Surviving is dealing with what comes your way.
If unsure of your place in life be comforted by the fact,
You are not the only one to have doubts, be scared, or want to give up.
What matters is you don't.

Ise Obomhense

Confetti Blossom

I switch on the ignition of the Honda,
parked on the driveway beneath over-arching
boughs of flowering cherry,
the April sun smiling from a cloudless sky.
A gust of wind springs up,
a fleeting flurry, a passing
Edinburgh squall, a burst of excitement.
And I am suddenly engulfed in blossoms,
a blizzard of pink confetti, a floral snowstorm.
Screened by a veil of glass, in wonderment
I sit, transported, as in a bridal chariot
upon my wedding day, setting out
to the shrine at Yokohama
for the ceremony of souls.

Norman Bissett

An Angel's Wing

After you left, I found an angel's wing.

I knew it wasn't mine
not even half of me could have aspired to such beauty.

When you left, although you didn't say,
I could tell you were injured: you were sad
with a smile, and you bore me -
bore me with all my troubles.

You listened,
you nodded,
you were there; with a warm and loving face.

You were there,
for me.

You told me you would be there.
You told me you would be there
for me.

You asked nothing of me -
nothing -
you gave everything -
everything -
everything of yourself
to me.

I can't think what I gave to you.
I can't think what I could have given to you
except, perhaps, your need to be needed:
that wasn't very much,
that was nothing.
I gave you nothing.

After you left
I felt lifted, refreshed, restored, unburdened,
free.

After you left,
I found an angel's wing,
I knew it wasn't mine.

Diana Mudd

You've Won!

Are you fearful of what you will leave behind?
Have you regrets of deeds left undone
or wasted opportunities?
Feelings towards others that were left unsaid
or deliberately wronged people without showing remorse, for . . .

If you can leave the world a better place than when you entered it,
then you've won

If you can leave the world after you have given your all,
then you've won

If you can leave the world when you have seen nature's beauty,
then you've won

If you can leave the world having lived every minute
then you've won

For it's never too late for change
Nor seize the moment before it's gone
To say 'I love you' from your heart
or be sorry and mean it, for . . .

If you can leave the world having helped others along the way,
then you've won

If you can leave the world when you have laughed and cried,
then you've won

If you can leave the world waving farewell to good friends,
then you've won

If you can leave the world knowing what's to come,
then you'll always win.

Derek Dobson

Reach Out

The morning breaks and how delightful
Reach out to greet another day
Start the day happy and joyful
As you meet others along the way

If for some reason
There is acquaintance
To be renewed for affection
Greet and be cheerful without reluctance

The gift of life is precious and is worth appreciating
Reach out to others in love, affection and consideration
Showing off the Creator's limitless dimension is uplifting
Reach out and show the world of people the Creator's
Powerful spirit of devotion.

Olive McIntosh-Stedman

Pookie

Pookie, an old mongrel, was abandoned without care
He found himself without the love that once was always there
He'd been a happy puppy, in a family he thought good
They took him out for walkies, treating him the way they should
But then he got run over but survived though very lame
And found the family didn't want to love him quite the same
So out he went like rubbish dumped upon a busy street
Where traffic was a death trap and a nightmare to defeat
But Pookie hobbled over, dodging death along the way
A hungry little mongrel who had only strength to pray
As night-time came his whimpers were a sign of sad despair
He missed the warmth and comfort of a home no longer there
He shivered as the night cold wrapped around his sorry frame
And huddled in a doorway just in case somebody came
His dinner had been scraps he'd found outside a garden gate
Not much to keep him going but he ravenously ate
Then eyes closed tight, the thought of home just made him want to cry
He felt the only choice he had was just curl up and die
But Pookie prayed that he'd be found and loved though he was lame
In spite of all his pain and grief Old Pookie was the same
Then early in the morning as the sun began to wake
A man who walked on crutches stopped and gave his paw a shake
'You look a bit like me,' he said, ' a little lame and old.
Why don't I take you home old lad, at least you'll not be cold.'
And so old Pookie followed him to find that love still shines
The man gave him his heart and soul and very happy times
So when life seems impossible and much too hard to bear
Remember dear old Pookie and the faith he had in prayer.

David Whitney

All For Jay

How do you categorise the people around you?
For you have no knowledge of who they are
Just faces in the crowd that pass you by
Until you need them, then they try

To ask around to help your child
Is not an easy thing to do
But to meet such individuals
Is such a blessing
Thank you

My son who has special needs
Needed a helping light
And the people around us, of Dunfermline
Made his future bright

It started as a family project
But that was not to be
Everyone joined in
To set my baby free

These individuals are special
And they have a big heart
We would have never got there
If they hadn't taken part

Margaret Pow

A Wish For Your Future

May all you wish for yourself come true
And every day have *some* sky that's blue.
May contentment stay close by your side
Along new paths as your faithful guide.

May those you meet return your smile,
May courage and quiet mark every mile.
May all you wish for yourself come true
At this time of life as you start anew.

Anne Everest

You Are

You are the morning brightness of each day
The sun of the lightness on display
The warmth of the glow
In the smile that you show
You are the gentle touch of insurance
The spoken words of assurance
You are the strength of the rock
You are the safe keeper of your flock
Single, unique and one of a kind
Aware of all around you, and never blind
One away from the crowd
So look at yourself and be proud

Terry J Powell

Need

I flee from regression
and from acute depression
I need a dose of redemption
to enable my mind's revolution
to make a new resolution
that brings forth a new evolution
of my mind, spirit and soul.

Debra Ayis

Don't Sit Alone

Don't sit alone with nothing to do
Get out and about, meet others like you
Everyone has a time, when it seems no one will care
If you find someone and talk, your troubles you'll share
It's no good us sitting behind our own wall
Someone's got to give in and make the first call
Much nicer to turn a dull day into fun
By helping yourself and helping someone
So next time you feel shut up in walls four
Put on your coat and knock on a door
You may find who answers turns out in the end
To be more than a neighbour, a jolly good friend.

Patricia Taylor

Untitled

My dear God! Will you teach me to have faith in You,
What is it in my life that I do not yet do?
Is it so that my soul up to You it must gaze
And so pass on to You grateful rivers of praise?

You have promised that You will not leave us alone
And take care of us while looking down from Your throne!
You have sent us Your Spirit as our divine guide,
In this way in our souls You will always abide!

After this maybe I cannot write anymore,
Though my thoughts shall be guided through Your open door!
To allow me to reach for Your infinite love
So that I may love You through Your grace up above.

Zoltan P Dienes

Thank You
(For Toni - thank you for everything)

To give as you have given, takes a love
Hallowed by a special kind of grace,
For the devotion you have bestowed,
Is a blessing that has moved my heart
In ways you cannot know.

How much care resides therein
All for me, you have so freely done,
In each, your unspent heart a message sends
Of care to which no words may match,
And my thanks may never end.

Your kindness I will not soon forget,
But held with gratitude within my heart,
A little piece will remain behind
In the dream that one day
I may touch someone's life
Just as you have touched mine.

Vicki Morley

Two Hearts Will Be One!

During this day your hearts will be one,
As you enter your life together.
And with the love of Christ all around,
You'll be spiritually guided forever.
With such love and such peace,
Flowing through our hearts.
Your love was planned by our God,
Right from the very start.
It's a special day for the both of you,
For our God has truly planned,
The perfect wedding shared with friends,
Created by His hands.
With Him now keeping an eye on you,
Your future will always be.
Guided by our God of all,
For all eternity.

Tracey Farthing

Aren't I The Lucky One?

It's a hazy, early dawn mist
that greets me the morning;
but soon it will fade and then reveal
a summer's day in all its glory!

Passion flowers spread like vine
clinging to the fence and pines,
displaying every flowering bud;
showing all the world their love.

The scent of honeysuckle fills the air.
There is new life bursting everywhere!
Aren't I the lucky one -
to be here in the midst of all this?

Thank you, who gave me sight
so I may see the blossom on the trees!
Thank you - who gave me ears
that I may hear the sounds of life!

What a joy to be a part
of nature's wondrous works of art.
Aren't I the lucky one - but not alone for I can share
a miracle that is everywhere!

Ros Heller

Candle

Glowing in the essence of a vigil
Bringing enlightenment into darkness
Warmth and fragrance into cold reality
Glimmering soft, slow and mellow, its
Illumination travelling at the speed of light
A glow in a metaphysical, transient form of life
Touching substance: dispelling formless night
There is a timeless time and in the passing
There is beauty, joy, comfort and sorrow
Conviction, hope and prayer by candlelight
Each temporal moment is consumed
In burning wick and waxen vapour
In flickering eye and faltering flame
Delicate and vulnerable in the restless air
My reflections in a spiral thread of prayer.

Kevin Power

Be Still And Know That I Am God

I was lost in a magical dream, a stunning vision from the great beyond
the master of all time, was holding me by the hand
explaining to me directly, now all your questions will be answered
those perplexing imponderables, that wracked the mind and soul
He looked at me with loving kindness, I was mesmerised by His
radiant eyes
I am your real Father, now you see me for the first time
no thing that was ever hidden, lacked a reason or a rhyme
He showed me the big screen, where He replayed the moments
of my life
translucent glories overshadowed all my hurts and pains
my eyes filled with tears as I realised all His loving care
I broke down with joy and called out, 'Abba, you were always there.'
Then I was shown all those dreams I'd thought I had been denied
and much to my chagrin I saw the disasters that would have befallen
if all these cherished wishes meant putting my will before the Lord
'You tried to measure happiness with the ruler of profit and gain and
failed to see the miracles in the simple span between you and me
for I was the hidden architect who designed the blueprint of your life
no good thing was withheld, you were unaware of all My blessings.'
And I couldn't answer, as the evidence was laid before my
incredulous eyes
He smiled with grace and honour, I was struck by the light of
His countenance as He quietly and gently whispered,
'You saw a little . . . I saw it all.'
I came away completely humbled and chastened to my core
my heart was filled with wonder, my spirit will never be
the same anymore
and then I was awakened by morning sunlight streaming its golden
rays and a song thrush was whistling and warbling eternity's
eternal refrain
my breathing was relaxed and I was filled with soothing calm
and I can tell you my true and faithful friend,
I've seen Heaven on the other side of the rainbow.

Peter Paton

The Bird

The bird on her golden perch, strained her neck and bent her head
To look around and down,
'You should never try to fly,' her master said.

The master had a little son, who opened the tiny chain
'Tie me oh boy lest I fall,' cried the bird but in vain
The boy was but only a kid; he could not undo what he did
And he left the bird unchained.

A howling wind came rushing in
Rocking the golden stand
Losing her grip, the bird fell down
Frightened and out of her mind.

The wings on her back trembled and shuddered
But what for, the bird never knew,
She dared to look up and there she saw
Her kith and kin in the blue
Flying and diving and soaring in the sky
Like kites without thread
She picked up her wings to join her folks
In the sky over her head

The master came running with chain in hand
Waving to his pet in the sky
She is not looking back, she is not looking down
To the chains she bade goodbye.

Santwana Chatterjee

Reflection

Would you really live your life again, amend events and the
power of conception
What lights would you turn off without exception?
Which sunsets would you brighten, what would you heighten?
We all dream in a cloud of regret, ponder actions we would
rather forget
I too sit and dream in reflections, bounced back from my
conscious inception
Music plays and stirs reminiscence, sowing my own seeds
of repentance
Why do I sink into this futile status, as if we could direct such
a pointless hiatus?
My days drift on in flows and tides, missing the point in every stride
I'm sat round a table 'midst whisky or gin listening to Cliff and
The Beatles again
Each one of us sips a low or a high; we can't rub them out
however we try
How gross to be affected and so deep in thought, what a pointless
ship in an improbable port
Wouldn't it be nice though to travel back, shuffle your cards and
change the pack
I will breathe deeply now and shed a tear because I can't change a
thing, just as I feared
Tomorrow I could be sober, in tune with my brain, to tell myself never
come back here again.
If only the past was left alone, never to bother me when left on my own
So what of the future as life slows down, will I still want to stop and turn
it all around?
Who knows or really even cares, it would appear future and past are
inseparable layers
What is pointless life or events, or what is real and to what extent?

John Foster

Just Another Day

I am sitting here on a rainswept day looking through a window
A murky looking day to sit and ponder will the rain relent?
Will the weather change? Where shall I go with goodwill and intent?
As I sit and gaze in awe at the scene seen through a window

A wonderful sight to greet us as the curtains glide away
A feeling of importance felt above the valley below
Visions will surround us as the wildlife moves some you know
Still the wind blows hard, the rain will fall for it is just another day

One morning may be different, when the sun shines through the day
A brand new scene so far away, fields with flaxen hair
Green trees will caress the landscape when all is calm and fair
With the wind and rain relented the sun shines through the day

As bumblebees fill their sacs from flowers grown outside
Birds and bees search for food while flying on the wing
The fields of corn sway in the breeze and birds will always sing
Then rabbits hurry from their holes, squirrels, nuts will hide

The sun will shine high as warm may feel the day
A feeling of contentment as I walk the fields of grass
Lying in the meadows, trekking through a pass
Tomorrow comes with wind and rain and it is just another day

J Barker

Life's Route

Please don't follow in my footsteps
You don't know where they may lead
And no matter what I have to say
My every word, please do not heed

In life we're individuals
And don't have to follow suit
You are given certain choices
And follow your own route

It's good to have a person
To help you choose the road to take
But you need to explore it on your own
And learn by each mistake

If life was made too easy
You'd get lost along the way
Unable to make your own choices
From the right road, you could stray

If you try to keep a level head
And think each problem through
In time each one will be resolved
And it will be all down to you

Don't get me wrong, I will give help
But I will not take the lead
I want to help you get the start
In life that you will need

A start in life in which
You'll make choices right and wrong
A life which you're in charge of
A life where you feel that you belong

Julie Preston

A Married Couple's Re-Avowal

(Husband to wife)
'To you my wife, I give my life,
As before and evermore.
From mountain top to ocean shore,
I'll sing your praises loud and clear,
And tell the world my love's sincere.

For you my wife, there'll be no strife.
I promised you, with wedding kiss,
Contented life, eternal bliss.
I sign, seal and declare anew,
My love forever, all for you!'

(Wife to husband)
'Oh husband mine, with zest you shine.
With your strength you always lead,
To see us through our times of need.
Your praises forever will I sing,
To me you are, a mighty king.

Oh husband mine, through my lifetime,
I'll love and cherish with all my heart.
And dread the time when we must part.
I sign to say with promise true,
All my love is just for you.'

Brian Kelly

The Silver Lining

When the dark tunnel stretches ahead
And at the end you see no light,
Life then reaches its lowest ebb
One has no will to continue the fight.

But life is not a bed of roses and
I am sure was never meant to be,
There is light at the end of every tunnel
Have faith, lift your eyes and you will see.

The whole of our life is a challenge
A gauntlet thrown down by God,
And He expects us to pick it up,
Not leave it lying on the sod.

Face the future, accept the challenge,
God's help is there if you ask,
Believe me you will never walk alone
No matter how difficult the task.

But try to smile through your troubles
Look and find the silver lining in the cloud,
And if your smile makes someone feel better
Then of that you can be proud.

R H Quin

Let Love Do The Rest

Knowing leads to pain
And joy
But never to wasted moments

For we can all do with the lessons
Of strength
Of endurance
Of support

For that is what we are here for
To learn
To love
To endure

The suffering of a child is not a small thing
For they feel everything
And know not how to shut down
That must be learned over time
By observation
By oppression
By dictation

Remember you when such a thing happened
What words did you crave
When the darkness fell
And your world ended

Use that as a template
Use your own words
And let love do the rest

Ann-Marie Spittle

Numbers

I was useless at maths at school.
Numbers beat me as a general rule.
Words I could trap at the end of my pen,
put them precisely in place and then
write a report or express my soul.

But numbers fled like scattered sheep.
I never found the way to keep
them in the place where they should be.
They ran from the page to the hills and trees.
Yes, maths was a mystery dark and deep.

The only maths I really know
is that two into one will only go,
when love is the bond to keep them together,
in grief and joy, in sun and foul weather.
For love is the answer to the problems of life,
when it lives in the hearts of husband and wife.

Bernard Fyles

Empathy

A bird sang in our garden as twilight fell
what species it was, I could not tell
but its song filled my darkening soul with light
and saw me all through the night

Came moon and stars to keep me company
and the bird, still it sang, as if just for me,
a song showing pictures of us to my inner sight
that saw me all through the night

Closer the dawn and a fear, come what may,
that even the bird could not soothe away;
moon and stars could but leave me to a plight
haunting me all through the night

Among the sun's first rays, I sought a smile;
the bird, typically, came that last mile
till I found peace and hope enough in a leafy sky
to see me through till my turn to die

Among even love songs heard or yet to hear,
none will sound sweeter to my ear
than of a bird whose species I could not make out
that once sang in our garden all night

Come the longest night of all, I'll go there again
and, together, we'll give the songbird a name

R N Taber

Angels

Truth is so often unidentified,
For fiction is so much easier to discern,
Leading us along a pathway of paper roses,
Fantasy replaces fact and fact equals fiction.
Do we follow fairies or do we follow angels?
Fairies flitter and flutter
And their tinkling bells give us meaningless pleasure.
Their beauty is unbelievable and the pleasure
That we feel is a fantasy world of shallow dreams.
The voice that's rarely heard is patience,
It takes a back seat, quietly watching,
Waiting for a time when you'll stop believing
In fairies and need a life with richer meaning,
And that is when we learn to follow angels.

Joan Elizabeth Blissett

In This Hour

In this hour of deepest grief,
It's in the Lord we can believe
To give you understanding and hope,
To guide you through and help you cope.

Please help them Lord to find the peace,
To lift this burden and bring happy release,
You'll never forget, but time will ease the pain,
You're feeling now and you will smile again.

Although this love has been taken you know,
The memory will live on in the heart and grow,
The time that you had will always be there,
It's God's way of saying, 'I'll help, I too do care.'

So in this time of your great sorrow,
Have faith and life will start to ease tomorrow,
Find support in all of those who care for you
And the faith and love of God will see you through.

Patrick J Horrell

You Would Not Know

I could not know in the long ago,
In the days that used to be,
That your primroses sweet in a bunch so neat,
Would set my tired spirit free.
I am there once again down memory lane,
By a bridge with a pool so deep,
With the fragrance of primroses sweetly there
Clothing the bank in a dress so fair,
And the silver of fish as they swish at my feet,
Making a scene that is quite complete.
I am young, if not fair, as at ripples I stare,
As the stone from my fist I let fly,
I am filled with delight, as are birds in full flight
As they twist and they turn,
Ere they soar out of sight.
And the ripples they spread as the stone falls like lead
Just a plop, then a soft seeming motion,
I would count - one - two - three,
My heart filling with glee,
If a fourth made it seem like an ocean.

You just could not know where your primroses grow,
And your kind thought 'A few will I gather,
It will brighten their day, and will have much to say
About kindness and will make them feel gladder'.
When spring days are gone,
With wild flowers and birdsong,
In memory they live once again dears,
It is kind folk like you that make them come true
For they came at a time when I felt rather blue.
So may those that you love look down from above,
To give you such joy, passing measure,
For the ripples that flow, they grow and they grow,
Giving old folk sweet memories to treasure.
You have cast your small stone,
And the ripples have grown,
To give courage, with no place for sorrow,
This will stay in our hearts for always and aye,
And return to give you joy tomorrow.

J Hammond

Deep Despair

Who knows when dark depression, may overtake the mind,
When perhaps traumas in the family, mean that peace is left behind.
It seems that every waking moment, holds dark foreboding dread,
At night somehow it's worsened, one quivers sleepless in their bed.
'Pull yourself together,' advice offered yes . . . by some,
Maybe it's well-meaning, yet still some hurt is done.
Sinking ever lower, then come suicidal thoughts,
'Try and count your blessings,' but all is seen as noughts.
None can ever know, just how another feels,
For none are in their shoes, so reality it conceals.
Since changes in the brain, have physiological effects,
So psychology is altered, which everything affects.
Without medical intervention, from this state it's hard to rise,
No matter what the situation, or opinions that seem wise.
Support and understanding, and patience sufferers need,
With prayers from many sources, for the treatment to succeed.
Jesus He had moments, when depression filled His soul
When despair was overwhelming, His world a yawning hole.
God made Man this person, as human as us all,
He identifies with suffering, for this He did befall.
So for each and every heartache, in whatever we may feel,
Christ is there for always, for this truth He does reveal.

Cecilia Skudder

Untitled

Hold on to your dream,
Don't let it die,
Look for the rainbow,
Not the cloudy sky.
The twinkling star,
Lights the darkest night,
These joys of each day
Make the future bright.

The vicious waves of the ocean,
Soothe when the sea is calm,
The sun melts your heartache,
Yet keeps your love warm.
Rain washes away sadness,
Fills life's flowing stream,
Enrich each day with a smile,
To fulfil your dream.

E M Gough

A Purpose-Driven Life

What is my purpose, what is my aim?
While I am here on this earth;
God knows my purpose, God alone knows
He planned, too, the day of my birth.
God fashioned me by His own design,
Gave me His word for a guide;
Sometimes I question why things occur,
Yet, for my redemption, Christ died.
Why am I here, what am I to do?
Jesus alone holds the key;
I seek the purpose of life on Earth,
God prepares for eternity.

We meet, sharing, drawing others in;
Part of God's family on Earth,
With praise and prayer, honouring His name
God blesses beyond worldly wealth.
His Spirit guides when seeking His will
Nourished by bread and by wine,
Going in His name, sharing 'good news'
Each person a part of the vine
Bearing fruit, nurturing the lonely, lost,
Helping and showing the way
To love and cherish all humankind
Serving one another each day.

Growing weary I long for the time
An ending of suffering and pain;
God's strength upholds, brings new hope and peace,
Rejoicing in sunshine and rain.
This is my purpose; Lord help me grow,
Bloom by your unending grace,
Then bring me home to the Father's House
To meet Jesus there, face to face.

Joan Heybourn

Higher Than High

You have lifted me high,
higher than high.
You are my inspiration,
my heart's desire.
Let me exult you Lord,
lift you high
higher and higher,
let me soar
with the wings of a dove,
higher and higher.
Lift me to the heights,
higher and higher.
You have lifted me high.

Penny Kirby

God's Promise

Once again Your arms are there
'Midst all the pain and tears,
Your promise stands forever Lord
And helps dispel our fears.

We feel Your strength around us
And Your love that we can share,
We know You won't forsake us
We know You're always there.

Sometimes we doubt Your presence
When we are really frail,
Somehow we know You carry us,
Your love will never fail.

Take away these fears Lord,
And make us one with You,
Whatever we are suffering
Your love will see us through.

Anne Smith

My Little Nan

(Tribute to poet Edna Gosney)

Everybody knows her as my little nan,
We share a bond that not many will ever have.
I will always remember her warm loving eyes,
For those who knew her, her kind heart never came as a surprise.

She was never really keen on little girls until I came along,
She took a shine to me and loved it when I sang the snowman song.
With effort and patience she taught me to spell
And even tell the time as well.

My little nan had the ability to make people laugh,
Most of the time it was from things that she'd done that were so daft.
She had a passion for poetry, crosswords and a good book,
But, oh my word how she hated to cook.

Her memories back from when she was a young girl,
My brother and I loved the stories she would tell.
We would sit either side of my nan together
And could listen to her voice telling stories forever.

She always used to say to me,
'You are my Kelly and always will be.'
I am proud to have had a nan who was so kind,
Another lady like her I will never find.

She was not just a nan but a best friend too,
She was always so proud of the crazy things I chose to do.
I know my little nan knew how much I loved her,
Nothing will change that but how I will miss her.

There's just one thing I want to say,
It probably won't make any sense to you today.
My little nan please don't forget our pact,
We'll meet again I'm sure of that.

Kelly Gosney

Positivity

Look at the bright side
It's something you should do
It's a positive way of thinking
It'll stop you feeling blue

I used to be a pessimist
It almost made me ill
I was told a pharmacist could help me
They said the answer's in a pill

The answer's not there really
Chemicals just mask the pain
Because deep inside your psyche
You still feel the strain

My answer's a bit more drastic
You must begin each day with hope
Keep smiling at the world
And you'll find it's easier to cope

It's helped me realise there's a future
It's exciting and it's bright
My life's a new adventure
Full of relish and delight

Andrew Lewis

I See God's Love

In softly flowing clouds
soaked in moist sweetness
in mellifluous notes
seeped in the wind
and the twinkle that shines
in the smiling eyes
I feel God's love
in the tender touch of the
wanted caress
in the heat of the hands
as they press
in the rustling of the
blossoming tree's dress
I hear God's love
in the voice of a friend
in the rhythm of the rain
as it gently descends
in the fading winter waves
as spring approaches
and hibernation ends.

Anjum Waim Dar

I Should Know, Being Old

I should know, being old,
Of how my world began,
With prehistoric creatures
That have enlightened Man.
The animals that roamed the Earth
In vast numbers, you'll agree,
Really have indeed surprised
The likes of you and me.

I should know, being old
Of how the world evolved,
From prehistoric creatures
To how early Man first solved
The art of primitive survival.
For flint, stone and hunting knife
Became the need of every man
The basic principles of life.

I should know, being old,
Of how my universe unfurled,
Through all the different ages
When great statesmen ruled the world,
From kings and queens of many lands
To the presidents of today;
And I would wish with all my heart
That peace might find a way.

I should know, being old,
Of what the future brings,
With discoveries of other worlds
And of all the many things
That Man has now invented.
So let my world keep turning
For endless years to come
And be prolific in your learning.

Because, I should I know being old.

Maureen Alexander

Bright Side

If everything around you now,
Were to vanish all in one;
Would there still be anything,
You'd really wish you'd done?

Life is short and sometimes sad,
So we should live it for each day,
And for the pleasure of the company,
Of the people on the way!

It's better if we take the chance,
To be happy for one week,
Than spend a lifetime with a heavy heart,
Never finding what we seek.

You'll have regrets along the way,
But on this I've never lied,
I'd rather regret something I've done,
Than to always wish I'd tried!

You make me laugh and make me smile,
But mostly chill me out,
This is, I find, a priceless gift,
I've been too long without!

You seem, like me, to be confused,
But on the way we'll mend,
Until this tower is rebuilt,
I'm glad that you're my friend.

I hope you have a happy day
And hope it lasts a while,
Life can be a damn sight worse,
If you forget to smile!

Omen

Message Of Hope

Please leave a 'Message of Hope', remember to say
When from this earthly life, I silently slip away,
I will donate my organs for which sick folk pray,
Helping others to live again, in a normal way.

A body in a coffin, just think, will eventually decay,
Or even disappear in a crematorium way.
Your 'Message of Hope' will brighten someone's day,
Bringing joy and miracles, please, take a Donor Card today!

Stella Bush-Payne

The Eternal Dreamcatcher

'Moonlight Becomes *you*',
as millions of stars smile down from the heavens,
twinkling as they dance to Your rhythm,
in this 'orchestrated' world where 'destiny' lies,
playing a different kind of 'Soul' music!'

'Sweet, beautiful dreams' are those when You come to visit,
the essence of Your presence engulfing my being,
filled me with Your warmth and love,
sharing my intimate secrets and thoughts -
whilst renewing my 'spirit' and reciting my passions, ambitions
                                                                    and dreams,
whispered on the 'wings of a prayer' to reach You in the night
                                                          sky above!'

'You are the answer to my prayers -
You wipe away my tears and take away my fears,
holding my hand and walking with me,
'In the Light' every step of the way along the path of life.
Until reaching the 'Fountain' of Your Blessing,
where I can bathe in infinite peace!'

'Your music is forever embedded in my soul,
when during the stillness of the night,
I dance to a different tune,
the one that was written for me in the stars, long ago,
to prepare me for the 'Quickstep' into Eternity,
with the dancing partner of my dreams' -

'The Eternal Dreamcatcher'!

Lisa S Marzi

The Wonderful Gift Of Life

The wonderful gift of life,
from a blade of grass to a tree,
from an insect to an animal
and far more wonderful you and me.

Animals can see the beauty around
and hear another's call,
but we have a wonderful brain
and can ponder on it all.

We have hands to make things
for our use and pleasure
and a brain to create things
we can keep and treasure.

Write music, poetry and books
on everything under the sun,
travel, natural history,
to 'how is it done'.

We can go back in time through memory,
or dream of better days;
and we will live forever
so the good book says.

Sometimes nature seems to error,
a baby is deformed or blind,
or is it just part of God's plan,
to teach us to be kind?

Whether we are rich or poor,
whether we are weak or strong,
this life is a testing period,
before we join the heavenly throng.

No one is singled out
for joy or troubles,
life is like a cookie,
it's just the way it crumbles.

The saint and sinner,
are equal in God's eyes,
one must try to be good
and the other not to despise.

If pain or poverty is our lot,
that we must patiently bear;
if we are blessed with health or wealth,
with less fortunate we should share.

The gift of life is wonderful
and for us to enjoy,
we must not abuse it,
or seek to destroy.

Violet Astbury

Blessings

Lord, while I sit and wonder
What lies in store for me,
I count the many blessings, Lord,
That I receive from Thee.

I marvel at the glories, Lord,
Created by Thy hand,
Of all the wondrous sights around,
In this Your beauteous land.

I thank You for the lovely days
You send us without measure -
Of all the lovely trees and flowers
That we on Earth can treasure.

I thank You for these hands of mine
And the gift to use them too,
That they may work so tirelessly
To praise and honour You.

If I forget to thank You, Lord,
for the blessings You bestow
Upon us, each and every day,
You'll remember us, I know.

Judith Herrington

Counting Blessings

We must count our blessings and name them every day!
This can be a constant prayer in a way!
It is thanking our Lord as we go about in the world each day.
There is so much gloom and despair round about!
The news on our TV and radio and also newspapers shout it out.
What can we do to make some difference in life?
Each and every one of us has a chance in this,
So to count our blessings we should not miss!
The most important thing we should not forget,
That God loves us all is the best blessing yet!
We hope our life in this world can be a blessing too,
As we meet others and in church say, 'God be with you.'

Joyce Hallifield

The Tree Of Life

The tree of life has branches two,
From stem of birth it spreads its growth.
So short the branch of mortal life,
So long our immortality.

The branch of soul's eternity
Will rise into infinity -
Mysterious concept for mere human minds,
Until God's revelation.

Jean Jackson

Keep Smiling

Look in a pool on a summer's day,
Your face is bright and gay,
Then look again in winter,
You're old and weary and grey,
So smile when you're feeling troubled,
Let the world know you're feeling fine,
It may be a lie but believe me it works
And you'll get to the end of the line.
The midst of the tunnel's the darkest,
Press on and you'll see a small light,
Then the brightness will shine like the daylight
And then day is in sight!

Never forget to be thankful,
In life you were given a place,
If you can keep on smiling
And to the world put on a brave face,
You're halfway to winning, you entered -
Took part, keep a smile on your face
And love in your heart.

Goldatt Jankiewicz

Angel

If an angel flew a thousand miles to come and say to you
a warm and deepened thank you for sending me this card,
With wings so white and perfect and heart of such sincerity,
a warm and kindest thank you can mean so very much,
To touch upon a single note that says a word for you,
a deep and meaningful person the note would play so true,
An angel stands beside you to whisper out the words
thank you.

J Jezierski

Hope

I hope I march the final mile
When time runs out, at last
I hope that I can raise a smile
Until my die is cast
To never have to cause a frown
Upon a loved one's face
And not to be a nuisance grown
To go out in good grace
I hope I march the final mile
And not be dragged along
I hope I do it in good style
I hope my faith holds strong

Gordon Andrews

Your Sad Loss

It's not easy when you lose someone
But it's something we all go through
And at this sad time you'll sit there wondering, why you?
You'll feel every kind of emotion
But the guilt's always at the top
And you'll wonder if the pain and hurt will ever, ever stop.
I can tell you from experience,
I won't lie, the truth I'll tell.
It hurts and hurts and hurts so much
You'll think that you're in Hell.
But the time will come
And you will move on
But it will never be the same.
You'll cry a little, cry a little
Each time you hear their name.

Aubrey Abram

When I Am Gone

When I am gone
Try to think kindly of me
Of the times of laughter
Not the dark moods -
When I am gone.

When I am gone
Try to think of the kind acts I did
For family and friends
Not the bitter times of rows -
When I am gone.

When I am gone
Try to understand my unhappiness
The frustration of my life
Not being what I had hoped for -
When I am gone.

When I am gone
Try to be pleased for me
For being at peace
And remember the good times -
When I am gone.

Rose L Ashwell

Daybreak

Darkness fades, the stars slip silently away.
The gentle pale moon quietly says goodbye
Softly the early sea mist drifts away,
And rosy streaks bedeck the aqua sky.

Reflected in the calm sea far below
A mackerel sky predicts a lovely day,
And soaring overhead with raucous cry,
Wings tinged with pink, the seagulls greet the day.
Floating on thermals in the fresh new dawn,
Weaving, diving, calling, welcoming the morn.

Lovely, this hour before the world awakes
When nature's peaceful splendour fills the sky
Promising a glorious summer day
Awaking softly as a baby's sigh.

Barbara Dunning

When Amongst The Bluebells

When amongst the bluebells my feet with careful tread
Walk in the spreading woodlands, boughs cathedralled overhead.
The birds' sweet song as whispered breeze brings movement in the
trees.
The earthy smells, the dappled light, the buzzing of the bees.

A world of beauty, quite apart from daily cares and worry.
A time to dream, to stand quite still, away from constant hurry.
The calm descends to ease away all care from 'furrowed brow',
To be renewed, begin anew, it works, I know not how.

It's nature's way of setting right all wrongs and daily woes,
It lifts the spirit, soothes the heart, takes away the 'lows'.
Listen carefully to nature's sounds, see sights beyond compare.
It's a wonderful world where we all live, a world which needs much
care.

'When amongst the bluebells my feet with careful tread'
As I gaze in wonder, these words keep running through my head.
Not just amongst the bluebells but throughout this 'precious land'.
Our feet must pick their path with care, small footprints in the sand.

Try to make the least indent, don't crush the hidden leaf.
Try to leave it all 'as found', no rubbish in the street.
We have to tread our pathway but please proceed with care.
We have to leave this planet for all our kin to share.

For them to see the magic of each and every day.
For them to travel all our paths, see joys along the way.
Try to leave out heritage for those who follow on.
That they may love, as we do, the beauty and the song.

History repeats itself, so often you've heard say,
But only if we do our share to help it on its way.
When amongst the bluebells our feet with careful tread,
Walk in the spreading woodland boughs cathedralled overhead!

Patricia Marland

Last Journey

When the tide is going out
I'll take your ashes to the sands
And let them trickle through my hands
Into the tide as it goes out

And they will drift on seven seas
North and south and east and west
As if you lived then at your best
When they drift on seven seas

But the best of you that was
Shall stay with me
Locked in my heart without a key
Safe in the best that was

Paul Thompson

Christ The Light

Christ the Light, the way to show,
His Word, the truth that we should know,
To teach and train in righteousness
So that in us His fruits will grow.

Christ our Lord, the source of life,
Made holy through His death for us . . .
By His wounds we are forgiven,
Sanctified for a life in Heaven.

Cathy Mearman

Embodiments Of Love

Love is so many things
A person or a place
A feeling or a thought
It lives and it grows
While it feeds and receives
Love does so many things

Love is all around us
In both actions and words
In hugs and in tears
It inhales and it creates
While it soothes and excites
Love holds both rain and sunlight

Love is like a flower
Healing and refreshing
Fragrant and pure
It promises and it deepens
While it flourishes and blooms
Love is a bouquet of hope

Love is what lovers make
Enduring and vibrant
Courageous and true
It arrives and it returns
While it remembers and feels
Love is when two hearts meet

Caroline Skanne

God Found

Calling water, water, does not make it wet
experience tells me this is true, so I won't forget
a higher power called God has to be experienced too
when this has happened you'll know God's in you

please be open-minded and give this a chance
if you do I promise your faith he'll enhance
faith is the answer to all problems we have
God's grace is free to all just like His love

just like the blind man, Jesus gave him sight
opened his eyes, for the first time seeing light
from the darkness of my mind He did the same for me
showing me where I was wrong and setting me free

as I was dead in my life, He restored my sight
turning the darkness of sin into shining light
freeing me from turmoil, my soul to release
I thank Him daily and this I'll never cease.

Jim Barker

Für Elise

'Tis for little Elise
I yearn, I sing
'Tis only Elise
My heart can win
A tiny face
And dimpled smile
Yellow ringlets
All the while
For Elise, little Elise
I bring a flower
Plucked I swear
From a pastoral bower
I swear
'Tis for little Elise
I yearn, I sing

Note: Für (Ger.) means only.

Margaret Bennett

Support For The Ill Or Bereaved

May prayer and patience heal the souls
of those who look to Thee,
'Peace Be Still' was Thy command.
Upon Lake Galilee.
The one and only, Lord of Lords,
Forgive our every sin.
That strength and courage may prevail
To fight and glory win.

Owen B Duxbury

`

Who Am I?

I too have known great passion,
Happiness and joy
And all the many emotions
In every girl and boy.

The pride in winning prizes
And passing an exam
Or helping someone on their way
All make me what I am.

My love of dancing to sweet music
Or listening to a song
Which stirs your deepest feelings,
That's where I belong.

So when I pass beyond this Earth
I hope you all will say,
'She wasn't such a bad old stick'
And cheer me on my way
(With a glass in every hand).

Jeanette L Durk

We Are So Blessed

White knight in shining armour
I'm blessed by all that you've done
You have such loving kindness
That can come second to none.

This lonely heart is changing
As I draw nearer to you
My cup is running over
Because your love's so true.

You heard this fair maiden's call
As it flew across the sky
Oh! How the gods have blessed us
From their thrones above so high.

Send me now the pure white dove
That I can make haste to you
We'll then go to paradise
Such a treasure it is true.

White knight I am reaching out
To hold now your loving hand
Let us walk in ecstasy
Along the shore's golden sand.

See the gods smile down on us
Feel their very happy heart
Our union was pre-ordained
And the gods played a large part.

Can you feel their perfect love
Flowing now through our own veins?
Healing all that went before
Our loneliness and our pains.

C S Cyster

Getting On

I fell in love and I became
The sparkle of the sunshine on a dewdrop in the mist,
The thrill of the whisperings in the trees,
The tingle in the trill of the blackbird's crystal song.
I became the ultimate me.
And my being brimmed high with the meaning of life
Which ran, giggling, into my soul
So that all these years later that blackbird sings still
And the thrill of the tingle has never grown old.

Eileen Caiger Gray

Secret History

Courage makes heroes of us all
We use it to mask our fear
It is hidden beneath the surface
Waiting to be tapped into.

So when you think you've lost the battle
And there's no more fight in you
Courage spurs you on
Like an angel pushing you.

E Christie

Blessings

The wonders of our world we
see, whether it be the great
seas or little busy bees.
Great oaks tall or
babies small.
The moon and stars by night,
the sun by day.
A rainbow through the rain
like tears glistening and
falling from a heart of pain.
But there is a God who sees
and cares about even a little
sparrow who falls, and
knows how many hairs are on
your head, and all of the
tears that are shed from a
heart of pain.
He is your shelter from a
storm, your strength for
today, your hope for tomorrow.
Taste and see that the Lord is
all He promises to be, for you
and for me.

Rita Cassidy

Your Life - Your Space

There's more to life than work and stress
Following rules and saying 'Yes'
You're on this Earth for but a while
So enjoy your life and try to smile
When things get heavy and pull you down
Think of nature - it has no frown
There are no deadlines except man-made
Health's your goal *not* being paid!
There are places to see and places to go
So take things easier - sort of nice and slow
Do your job - don't get me wrong
But ease your tension and be strong
By saying 'No' and 'I'll do that later'
You're not on wheels - nor a 'dumb waiter'
When things get frantic and strife is around
Just lay back and listen to the sound
Of those with authority as they strive to please
The bosses *above them* on their bended knees
As a poet once wrote from his table and chair
'What is this life if full of care?'
We're on this planet for just one life
Don't make it shorter as with a knife
By worry and anger and fear and dread
Live this - your space - you're a long time dead!

Alan R Coughlin

Moulded

There are things in my life, Lord, I loathe and detest,
and some things I could change if I would.
Help me to desire nothing less than the best,
prepared to accept what I should.
For I know that the vessel you've moulded and pressed
one day you will call 'very good'.

Ken Miles

Will We Ever Learn To Be?

Denounce or admit
That the picture might be true,
The birth of us all
In a galaxy so blue.

Where the stars burn and ponder
On the wisdom of it all
And the sun shines down
And holds us all in thrall.

In a pre-atomic world
Where cavemen sit and stare
And ask the same questions
Of which we are aware.

This malleable universe
Where planets come and go.
Do we ever reach maturity?
Or build on what we know?

Will we ever learn to be?
Just be and not to care?
For past or future
We're neither here nor there.

Philosophers and priests,
Laymen and the young
Reach a certain point
And find they've just begun.

For the beginning was so small,
It's difficult to see
And the end is oh so distant
That what will be will be.

John Hobbs

My Little Flower

Roses are red,
Violets are blue,
Daffodils are yellow,
Daisies are white,
You are indeed my little flower,
For sure a delight,
Such a beautiful sight,
My little flower, beautiful and bright,
A little flower from a bud grows,
To be a beautifu bright flower
You a little girl from a baby have grown,
To be a beautiful girl,
Yes my beautiful little flower,
My beautiful angel princess,
Colourful and bright, a pure delight,
You are indeed a beautiful sight,
A pure delight,
My little flower Jordana,
You do certainly brighten up the day,
With your beautiful smile,
With your beautiful laugh,
My beautiful Jordana angel princess,
Just like a little flower,
So beautiful and delightful,
Yes, roses are red,
Violets are blue,
Daffodils are yellow,
Daisies are white,
You indeed Jordana,
My little flower,
My angel princess.

David J Hall

Flowers

How beautiful they are,
Rose, you stand out in a crowd.
Lily, you're such a petal,
Primrose, what a colour.
Violet, you're so cute.
Pansy, what a lovely face.
Iris, you are small,
But can be tall.
Daisy, how firm you have grown.
Ivy, not a flower,
But you do creep around.
You flowers say it all.

Iris Oldham

Louis And His Testimonial

'So you don't want me
Now that I'm getting old,
Though I'm a senior
Cat, so I've been told.
Long black fur
As smooth as silk is
Such a joy to behold.
Yes, I've always kept
Myself in shape
And done as I'm told.
My life is still precious
Though time is fast ticking away.
My time on Earth
Is limited so they say.
Then one day when
The gates of Heaven
Open wide for me
And my testimonial
Is presented for
All to see.'

'So you've never killed
A bird,' St Peter said
With a long spiritual grin.
'You're welcome within
And before you shear those sheep
Catch this large glass of gin.'

David Ashley Reddish

Forward Press Information

We hope you have enjoyed reading this book - and that you will continue to enjoy it in the coming years.

If you like reading and writing poetry drop us a line, or give us a call, and we'll send you a free information pack.

Alternatively if you would like to order further copies of this book or any of our other titles, then please give us a call or log onto our website at www.forwardpress.co.uk

Forward Press Ltd. Information
Remus House
Coltsfoot Drive
Peterborough
PE2 9JX

(01733) 898101